WELL BUILT MYCENAE

*The Helleno-British Excavations
Within the Citadel at Mycenae, 1959–1969*

W. D. Taylour, E. B. French, K. A. Wardle

FASCICULE 24

The Ivories
and objects of
Bone, Antler and Boar's Tusk

O. H. Krzyszkowska

Published and distributed by
Oxbow Books, Park End Place, Oxford OX1 1HN
Phone: (+44) 01865-241249, Fax: (+44) 01865-794449
Email: oxbow@oxbowbooks.com

Distributed in North America by
The David Brown Book Company
PO Box 511, Oakville, CT 06779
Phone: (860) 945-9329, Fax: (860) 945-9468
Email: david.brown.bk.co@snet.net

Website address
www.oxbowbooks.com

© Mycenae Publication 2007

All rights reserved. No part of this publication may be reproduced, or stored in a retrieval system or transmitted, in any form or by any means, electronic, mechanical, photocopying, recording or otherwise, in any part of the world, without the prior written permission of the copyright holders to whom requests for permission should be made at mycenaepub@aol.com

ISBN 978 1 84217 295 7

Printed in Great Britain at
Information Press, Eynsham, Oxford

CONTENTS

TEXT

Foreword   v

Introduction   1

Acknowledgements   2

Part 1. The Ivories   3
    Categories   3
    Materials   4
    Find Contexts and Chronology   6
    The Objects   16
    Workshops and Workshop Material   50

Part 2. Objects of Bone, Antler and Boar's Tusk   53
    Categories   53
    Materials   54
    Find Contexts and Chronology   55
    The Objects   62

Endnotes   79

Bibliography and special abbreviations   81

Context, pottery and photographic information   85

TEXT ILLUSTRATIONS

Figures

Fig. 1	General plan of the Citadel House Area.	5
Fig. 2	Ivories from Room 19 (those found in bowl marked *). Phase VII.	7
Fig. 3	Ivories from Room 31. Phase VII. For head **I-1** and lion **I-2** see Pls. 1–4.	8
Fig. 4	Principal ivories from Room II. Phase VII. **I-78** found over Room II (context 0829). For hippopotamus tusk **I-84** see Pl. 16.	10
Fig. 5	Principal ivories from Room 32. Phase VII floor deposit. For ivory cube **I-70** see Pl. 13.	11
Fig. 6	Ivories from Area 36. **I-38** from Phase VII floor 2; remainder found above floor 2.	12

Fig. 7	Selected ivories from Phase VIII deposits. See also figure-of-eight toggle **I-13** (Pl. 5), pommel **I-18** (Pl. 6) and indeterminate objects **I-53** and **I-54** (Pl. 9).	13
Fig. 8	Ivories from phases IX and X (**I-7**, **I-36** and **I-83**).	15
Fig. 9	Diagrams showing how (*a*) cube **I-70** and (*b*) wedge **I-73** were cut from tusk.	45
Fig. 10	Selected objects of bone, antler and boar's tusk from pre-phase VII.	56
Fig. 11	Selected objects of bone, antler and horn from phase VII.	57
Fig. 12	Selected objects of bone from phase VIII.	59
Fig. 13	Selected objects of bone and antler from phases IX, X and XI.	61
Fig. 14	Selected objects of bone and antler from phase XIV (Hellenistic).	62
Fig. 15	Selected objects of bone, antler and boar's tusk from mixed and surface levels.	63

Plates
(see p. 85 for explanation of Mycenae Archive photographic references)

Pl. 1	Ivory head **I-1**. *Top left* 85-R/7/10; *top right* 85-R/7/7; *centre left* 85-R/6/10; *centre right* 85-R/7/6; *bottom* neg. O. H. K.	18
Pl. 2	Ivory head **I-1**. *Bottom left* 85-R/6/5; *bottom right* 85-R/5/5.	19
Pl. 3	Ivory lion **I-2**. *Top left* 3300; *top right* neg. O. H. K.; *centre* 3366a; *bottom* 3365a.	22
Pl. 4	Lion **I-2**. *Top* 3365b; *centre* and *bottom* negs. O. H. K.	23
Pl. 5	(*a*) Figurine **I-3**, *left* 69/35/17/46, *right* 69/35/17/44. Cosmetic articles: (*b*) cosmetic implement **I-9**, 69/35/17/42; (*c*) pendant or toggle in shape of figure-of-eight shield **I-13**, *left* 60/35/11/4, *right* 60/35/11/5; (*d*) spoon **I-8**, 70/35/22/1.	28
Pl. 6	Pommels: (*a*) **I-17**, *left* 69-R/7/2, *right* 69-R/7/1; (*b*) **I-18**, *left* 60/35/7/35, *right* 60/35/7/36. Naue II hilt-plates: (*c*) **I-20**, 69/35/14/11; (*d*) **I-21**, 69/35/15/5.	30
Pl. 7	Appliqués: (*a*) 'dagger' **I-26** (upper surface), 64-R31; (*b*) moulding **I-28** Face A, 70/35/22/37; (*c*) moulding **I-28** Face B, 70/35/22/39; (*d*) moulding **I-28** Face C, 70/35/22/41; (*e*) oval attachment **I-29**, 70/35/12/42.	33
Pl. 8	Inlays: (*a*) **I-30**, 62-R175; (*b*) **I-31**, 62-R140; (*c*) **I-34**, 69-R/6/12; (*d*) **I-37**, underside, 62-R175; (*e*) **I-38**, upper surface (*above*) 70-R/5/9, underside (*below*) 70-R/5/11; (*f*) **I-43**, 62/35/8/18; (*g*) **I-46**, 62/35/8/17; (*h*) **I-49**, 62/35/7/20.	35
Pl. 9	Indeterminate objects: (*a*) rectangular slab **I-53**, 82/35/11/29; (*b*) segment with moulding **I-54**, 60/35/7/35; (*c*) segment with moulding **I-54**, 60/35/7/36.	37
Pl. 10	Partly worked ivories. Unfinished objects: (*a*) **I-60** upper surface, 62-R137; (*b*) **I-61**, 69-R/6/6; (*c*) **I-62**, 69-R/6/10; (*d*) **I-62**, 69-R/6/9; (*e*) **I-65**, 70/35/14/1; (*f*) **I-64** upper surface, 69/35/31/51.	39

Pl. 11	Partly worked ivories. Blanks: (*a*) **I-66**, 62-R175; (*b*) **I-67**, *left* 83-R/2/9, *right* 83-R/2/6; (*c*) **I-68**, 69/35/15/11.	41
Pl. 12	Ivory comb blank **I-69**: (*a*) Face A, 61/35/3/33; (*b*) Face B, 61/35/3/34.	42
Pl. 13	Partly worked ivory cube **I-70**: (*a*) 'main' Face E, 85-R/2/2; (*b*) 'inner' Face D, 85-R/2/4; (*c*) Base B, 85-R/2/5; (*d*) 'outer' Face (natural surface) C, 85-R/2/3; (*e*) Face F, 85-R/2/1. (See CD p. 257 for decayed 'top' Face A.) Fig. 9 (*a*) shows how **I-70** was cut from the tusk.	43
Pl. 14	Partly worked ivories. Tusk tip: (*a*) **I-71** Face A, 82/35/12/5. Large off-cuts: (*b*) **I-72** Face A, 69-R/6/4; (*c*) **I-73** Face A, 4/91-R/6; (*d*) **I-73** Face B, 4/91-R/7; (*e*) **I-73** edge a–d with pulp cavity, 4/91-R/8; (*f*) **I-74** Face A, 4/91-R/5; (*g*) **I-74** Face B, 4/91-R/3; (*h*) **I-74** Face C outer surface, 4/91-R/2.	46
Pl. 15	Partly worked ivories. Off-cuts: (*a*) **I-75**, 69/35/14/44; (*b*) **I-77**, 69/35/31/23; (*c*) **I-76** Face A, 69-R/6/7; (*d*) **I-76** Face B, 69-R/6/8; (*e*) **I-79**, 65/35/17/30; (*f*) **I-78** Face A, 84/35/5/14; (*g*) **I-78** Face B, 84/35/5/15; (*h*) **I-80**, 70/35/3/41.	47
Pl. 16	Segment of hippopotamus tusk **I-84**, *above* 83/35/2/18A, *below* 83/35/2/19A.	49
Pl. 17	Handles of bone and antler: (*a*) **B/I-1**, 62-R133; (*b*) **B-3**, 70-R/5/8; (*c*) **A-1**, 69/35/24/15.	65
Pl. 18	Bone pins and spatulae. Pins: (*a*) **B-4**, 69/35/20/10; (*b*) **B-11**, 69/35/23/2; (*c*) **B-12**, 69/35/6/10; (*d*) **B-17**, 69/35/24/5; (*e*) **B-18**, 82/35/5/35; (*f*) **B-19**, 65/35/15/61; (*g*) **B-20**, 65/35/14/40; (*h*) **B-21**, 65/35/11/36; (*i*) **B-22**, 65/35/15/39. Needle: (*j*) **B-27**, 69/35/31/59. 'Spatulae': (*k*) **B-28**, *left* 82/35/5/10, *right* 82/35/5/11; (*l*) **B-29**, 60/35/13/23; (*m*) **B-30**, 82/35/5/0.	66
Pl. 19	Bone tools: (*a*) **B-53**, 69-R/6/3; (*b*) **B-55**, 69/35/6/65; (*c*) **B-56**, 70/35/4/71; (*d*) **B-58**, 70/35/19/7; (*e*) **B-59**, 69/35/14/19; (*f*) **B-64**, 69/35/13/0; (*g*) **B-67**, 69-R/3/7; (*h*) **B-68**, 70-R/3/12; (*i*) **B-69**, 65/35/18/51. Horn core: (*j*) **H-1**, 70/35/20/25.	71
Pl. 20	Antler tools: (*a*) **A-3**, 70-R/16/3; (*b*) **A-6**, 70-R/4/1; (*c*) **A-7**, 70-R/5/14; (*d*) **A-8**, 70-R/6/2; (*e*) **A-10**, 69/35/31/39.	75
Pl. 21	Boar's tusks: (*a*) **BT-1**, 69/35/1/24; (*b*) **BT-2**, 69/35/31/74; (*c*) **BT-3**, 59/35/7/34; (*d*) **BT-4**, 69/35/31/21; (*e*) Room II group including **BT-9**, **BT-10**, **BT-12** and **BT-14**, 62-R169.	78

CD

The Ivories, **I-1** to **I-84**	103
Ivory Conservation at Mycenae	286
Objects of Bone and Horn, **B/I-1** to **B-75**, **H-1**	303
Objects of Antler, **A-1** to **A-17**	403

Objects of Boar's Tusk, **BT-1** to **BT-16** 435

Non Artifacts, **U-1** to **U-14** 455

Concordance 470
Context Lists 477
Full Data List 484
General Bibliography and Special Abbreviations 492

ADDITIONAL ILLUSTRATIONS ON CD

Plans
Phase VII 490
Phases IX and XII 491

FOREWORD

The ivory lion and the ivory head found in the Room with the Fresco during the last seasons of the Citadel House excavation are among the most remarkable finds from the area and are now key exhibits in the new Mycenae Museum display. While these are of unique importance in the study of Late Bronze Age sculpture, and are well known from illustrations in a variety of publications, they are far from being the only items of ivory discovered. Numerous off-cuts and partially worked pieces were found in two major storage contexts connected to the Cult Centre, in Room II at the south end of the Megaron and in Room 32, the storeroom beyond the Room with the Fresco. These are of equal interest for understanding the production of artifacts in ivory and also emphasise the status of the complex as a whole. The range of other items of ivory and of boar's tusk, bone, horn and antler includes a large number of both functional and decorative pieces which extend our understanding of Aegean craftsmanship. These objects were found in contexts representing almost all of the periods of use in the Citadel House Area, although the majority come from those sealed by the disaster at the end of Phase VII (*c*. 1230 BC). While the date of deposition is thus generally clear, the date of the *production* of any individual piece, remains a matter of discussion, as it does for most ivories in the Aegean world.

Lord William Taylour assigned all objects of these organic classes, whether finished, part finished or raw material, to Olga Krzyszkowska for study and they represented an important part of her PhD thesis. Since then study of the site and its stratigraphy by EBF and other members of the Mycenae publication team has permitted much greater precision about the contexts of discovery and associations. Dr Krzyszkowska's widely acknowledged expertise in this field has allowed her access to many groups of comparative material and enabled the identification of parallels from throughout the Aegean area.

In this definitive account, the third of the fascicules in this series devoted solely to the objects found, she has presented the objects according to material and typology and has discussed the contexts and find spots in a similar manner to Fascicule 21 (Mycenaean Pictorial Pottery) and 27 (Ground Stone). Part 1 is devoted to 125 objects of ivory which include carvings in the round, cosmetic articles and jewellery, other functional items and furniture decorations as well as indeterminate fragments, probably of finished objects, and pieces of partly worked ivory. The vast majority of these items are of elephant ivory although the presence of two strips of inlay and a large unworked segment of hippopotamus lower canine, remind us of the significance of this alternative material.

Part 2 focuses on 115 objects made from the more mundane, organic materials (bone, horn, antler and tusk) which were locally available and used to make decorative pins as well as functional items such as handles and piercing tools. The distribution of these objects is more even through the different strata and their frequency in each is a function more of the volume and type of deposit than of any historical significance. None of these categories, however, has been well served in the publications of Mycenaean settlement sites to date and they should provide a welcome addition to our knowledge of domestic and practical activities.

The account and discussion in the printed text is accompanied by representative illustrations of each class. Full details of every object including photographs and drawings are provided on the catalogue pages supplied and indexed on the CD-Rom. Our original intention was to provide microfiche as had been done for the earlier fascicules but following discussion with David Brown of Oxbow it was decided that this was no longer economically viable. The page numbering prepared for the fiche has not been changed nor have the cross references to fiche within the catalogue pages. A paper copy of these pages is filed in the Library of the British School at Athens and at Mycenae. Context information is given in the standard format used in all Mycenae fascicules. It includes reference to trench, year and unit number, phase, pottery date range, room or area. The index of codes and abbreviations can be found on p. 85. The general bibliography can be found on p. 492 while the specialized bibliography for this Fascicule is printed on p. 81.

Especial thanks are due to Rayna Andrew who has formatted the text and catalogue pages and prepared many reproductions of photographs and other illustrations with assistance from Graham Norrie. The Cambridge University Photography Service helped with negatives in formats no longer familiar. Photographs are largely the work of EBF, with some by WDT and OHK.

The original pencil drawings of the head and the lion are the work of Talbot Christie while Rosalind Thomas prepared the specialized illustrations of items with working traces. Frances Gleave is responsible for the excellent drawings on the find cards of the majority of the minor items. Most have been inked by Doniert Evely. Sibby Postgate has adapted her diagrammatic plan of the area for use in this fascicule. Diana Wardle has drawn and designed the cover illustration.

The assistance of the staff of the Mycenae Museum and Kim Shelton has been invaluable for correlating exhibition numbers for the objects published here. Trevor King and Gillian Smith of Micromedia have undertaken the creation of the CD-Rom.

Work on this fascicule has been supported financially by the Mediterranean Archaeological Trust established by Lord William Taylour and by private donations in memory of Alan Wace.

EBF/KAW October 2006

PLEASE NOTE: CORRECTION TO MYCENAE MUSEUM NUMBER PREFIXES

Throughout this Fascicule we have used MM as the prefix for the Mycenae Museum Accession Numbers; this should be BE. MM is the correct designation of the Exhibit Numbers, listed under the heading 'Display No.' on pp. 484–9.

INTRODUCTION

Ivories were first discovered at Mycenae 125 years ago. Unfortunately little is known about the context of either those found by Schliemann or by Tsountas[1] on the acropolis. They were not fully published and no work has been done on such archives as exist. Ivories were also found by Mylonas in various locations on the acropolis: these are known only through preliminary reports. For the most part, items made of bone and antler have gone entirely unremarked or else have been wrongly described as ivory. Fortunately, other groups of ivories from Mycenae have received better treatment. These include the ivories from the Shaft Graves, chamber tombs and last, but not least, from the Houses outside the Citadel. From these sources we gain many valuable insights into the development of Mycenaean ivory carving from its innovative beginnings in LH I–II through to its developed phase in LH IIIA–B. Indeed no other site on the mainland or Crete offers such a comprehensive range of datable material or such a wide variety of products. None the less, the lack of evidence from the acropolis represents a major impediment. Not only is the distribution of ivories within the palace and its dependencies unknown, so too is the location of possible workshops, attested indirectly through surviving offcuts, roughouts and waste pieces

Against this backdrop, the discovery of ivories in the Helleno-British excavations in the Citadel House Area on the south-west slope of the acropolis is of considerable importance. The items encompass carvings of the finest quality — the magnificent lion and the well-known head of a young man — and partly worked ivory in significant quantities. Objects of bone, antler and boar's tusk are also well represented. Moreover, their find contexts are well documented and securely dated. Most of the ivories come from phase VII (mid LH IIIB) deposits. While the new evidence from these excavations can never wholly offset earlier lacunae, it undoubtedly adds to our overall understanding of ivory use at Mycenae.

This fascicule is divided into two parts: the first deals with the ivories, the second with items of bone, antler and boar's tusk. In total there are 193 catalogued entries, representing about 240 individual items. The discrepancy arises because some original inventory numbers included more than one object, e.g. **I-30** (62-1658B) a group of 11 narrow inlay strips. In such cases it seemed sensible to retain the original excavation groupings. To assist the user, a letter prefix has been given to each catalogue entry. This indicates the material from which the item is made, e.g. ivories being identified by the letter **I** (**I-1** to **I-84**). Objects of bone (**B-1** to **B-75**), horn (**H**), antler (**A**) and boar's tusk (**BT**) are treated in similar fashion. The numbering is individual to the various subsections and not consecutive throughout the whole catalogue. Also included are 14 unworked specimens of bone (**U**), 13 of which were originally inventoried as small finds.

The catalogue in this fascicule is provided on CD-ROM only. Originally it had been intended to include microfiche and the catalogue pages were prepared for that format and numbered 101–98, 201–87, 301–98, 401–98. This *numbering* has not been changed, nor have cross references to *fiche* pages been adjusted. The catalogue includes a full description of each object, published references, comparanda and illustrations. The most important pieces are also illustrated in the text. The two parts of the text are set out in similar fashion, although the ivories merit more detailed treatment, both individually and collectively. At the beginning of each part, I explain the main categories of objects and contexts in which they were found. This is followed by a discussion of the individual pieces and their significance.

ACKNOWLEDGEMENTS

The study of this collection has spanned many years. Initial work was carried out as part of my doctoral research during 1978 and 1979, with supplementary study taking place in 1983. Selected ivories were re-examined in 1986, as part of a wider investigation into the use of hippopotamus ivory in the Aegean Bronze Age. At the same time, some of the antler tools were re-studied and compared with tool marks on glass ornaments. Although publication of the fascicule was then delayed, the intervening years have proved beneficial. I have been able to examine (and re-examine) many more ivories and undertake further analysis of the materials, their uses, and the many problems associated with workshop material. The contexts in the Citadel House Area are now much better understood, thanks to the work by Dr Elizabeth French. The fascicule was entirely re-written in autumn 2000, with minor additions and corrections added in autumn 2001. I have also incorporated new observations on the famous ivory head and magnificent lion, which were examined in the Mycenae Museum during September 2001.

A lengthy period of study inevitably produces many scholarly debts. Lord William Taylour generously entrusted this important material to me at a very early stage in my doctoral research. I deeply regret that he did not live to see the results published. My gratitude to Dr Elizabeth French and Dr Ken Wardle is no less, for without their help and guidance over the years this study could not have been produced. I am also extremely grateful to Mrs Diana Wardle for many profitable discussions and pertinent advice. I cordially thank Rayna Andrew for transforming my manuscript into the finished fascicule, complete with its many pages on CD-ROM. I owe a special debt to Dr Doniert Evely, who not only skilfully inked the drawings, but who also offered many valuable insights on craft technology. Mrs Helen Hughes-Brock has been a constant source of encouragement and has also provided vital information on glass working and jewellery. Dr Katie Demakopoulou greatly facilitated my studies into ivory and related materials, by showing me her finds from Thebes and by permitting me to examine published and unpublished objects in the National Museum, during her tenure as Ephor of the Prehistoric Collections. I am also indebted to the late Professor Klaus Kilian, for his generosity in allowing me to stay in the German Excavation House in Nauplion, and for inviting me to publish the Tiryns ivories, which offer important comparanda for those at Mycenae. To his successor Professor Joseph Maran I am grateful for bringing the Tiryns ivories to press. Many other colleagues have also helped by allowing me to study material, by asking searching questions, by providing urgent answers, or by offering much-needed encouragement. They include: Dr Maureen Alden, Mr Robert Arnott, Dr Vassilis Aravantinos, the late Professor J. L. Caskey, Dr Hector Catling, Dr Annie Caubet, Mr Brian Cook, Miss J. Lesley Fitton, Professor Louis Godart, Dr Anna Grammenou, Mr Sinclair Hood, Professor Spyros Iakovidis, Dr Imma Kilian-Dirlmeier, Dr Richard Laws (for the gift of a hippopotamus tusk), Dr Holley Martlew, Miss Athina Papadakis, Dr Sebastian Payne, Professor Ingo Pini, Mr Christos Piteros, Professor Jean-Claude Poursat, Dr Susan Sherratt, Professor Peter Warren and Dr Martha Heath Wiencke. To these and to any others, whom I have unwittingly omitted, I am most grateful. Last but not least, I thank my husband Major Antony Vickery, for many years of patience and unflagging support.

O. H. K.

PART 1. THE IVORIES

This part deals with 84 catalogued entries, representing about 125 individual items of ivory (see p. 1). Some are undoubtedly finished objects, but others are best described as 'partly worked ivory' — a miscellany of blanks, rough-outs, off-cuts and waste segments. The collection also includes more enigmatic pieces, occupying a shadowy zone between the finished and the partly worked. Some of these may have been abandoned during the course of manufacture, others may have been salvaged for re-use. Trying to make sense of individual items is often exceedingly difficult. Even among the finished objects we face dilemmas. Some pieces are unique, but relatively easy to understand; others are simply incomprehensible. Only about half of the pieces have safe parallels among other collections. Furthermore, combs and inlays aside, most pieces occur as singletons within the Citadel House Area. This fact also makes for difficulties in devising a suitable typology. Large numbers of similar objects are often easier to deal with than small disparate collections.

CATEGORIES

In his authoritative study, *Les ivoires mycéniens,* Poursat demonstrates that in functional terms most Mycenaean ivories fall into a few broad categories (Poursat 1977a, 17–18). These include cosmetic articles — combs, pyxides and mirror handles — often finely carved in low relief; inlays, appliqués and relief plaques, which belonged to wooden furniture or caskets, now lost; and finally various functional objects, such as pommels, usually undecorated. To these one should add carvings in the round, which are rare in the Mycenaean repertoire and which are usually unique pieces (Poursat 1977a, 45–6). Although I have attempted to present this collection under similar headings, these serve only as a broad framework. Indeed, given the difficulties outlined above, the assignment of specific objects often entailed a series of compromises, some less happy than others.

I-1 to **I-3**	**Carvings in the round.** These include the well-known head of a young man (**I-1**), a magnificent lion (**I-2**) and a small figurine of uncertain origin (**I-3**).
I-4 to **I-16**	**Cosmetic articles and jewellery.** None of the combs is decorated, nor are there examples of fine pyxides or mirror handles, which have been found almost exclusively in tombs. Indeed, apart from the cosmetic implement (**I-9**) the objects in this category are undistinguished.
I-17 to **I-25**	**Other functional items.** Most evidently served as components of objects made in other materials (e.g. pommels and hilt-plates: **I-17** to **I-21**). Others, like the 'acorn-shaped object' (**I-24**) are harder to understand, but belong to well defined Mycenaean types.
I-26 to **I-51**	**Furniture decorations.** Appliqués and inlays of various kinds.
I-52 to **I-59**	**Indeterminate fragments**, probably of finished objects.
I-60 to **I-83**	**Partly worked ivory.** Unfinished objects, blanks, rough-outs, off-cuts, waste segments.
I-84	**Hippopotamus lower canine.** Large segment, unworked.

Within each category, catalogue order is determined by type, find spot and date. For instance among the furniture decorations, all inlay strips are grouped together, followed by rosettes and lilies.

MATERIALS

Principal study of the collection was undertaken before criteria had been established for distinguishing between elephant and hippopotamus ivory (Krzyszkowska 1988; 1990). None the less, most of the finished objects are probably made from elephant ivory. Two inlay strips (re-examined in 1986) seem to be hippopotamus ivory (**I-33**, **I-34**). All of the partly worked pieces are certainly elephant ivory and provide invaluable insights into the methods used for sectioning tusks (Krzyszkowska 1992*a*). The large segment of hippopotamus lower canine, which (as preserved) bears no definite signs of tool marks, represents about one-quarter of a tusk. Its identification by the author in 1978 helped focus attention on the possible use of hippopotamus ivory in the Aegean Bronze Age, which is now extremely well documented (Krzyszkowska 1984; 1988).

The preponderance of elephant ivory in the Citadel House Area is consistent with the pattern observed among other collections from the Late Mycenaean period. From LB I onwards, elephant ivory became more widely available throughout Egypt and the east Mediterranean, which had a major impact on craft output and helped shape the character of local production centres (Krzyszkowska and Morkot 2000, 320, 324–5). It is certainly true in the Aegean where we find a sudden explosion of combs, pyxides, mirror handles and furniture plaques lavishly decorated in low relief. For products such as these elephant ivory was essential. But the question remains: once the advantages of elephant ivory were recognized in the Aegean, was there a deliberate attempt to acquire it in preference to hippopotamus tusk? Unfortunately we know next to nothing about the mechanisms of ivory acquisition and exchange in the LBA. While we may speculate that elephant ivory in Egypt and the east was largely — if not exclusively — under royal control, the status of hippopotamus ivory in the LBA remains unclear. Here it is worth re-iterating that there are no scientific means available for pinpointing the origin of tusks or worked ivory (Krzyszkowska and Morkot 2000, 320–1). Elephant ivory may have reached the Aegean from Africa via Egypt or from western Asia via coastal Syria (or even indirectly via Egypt, which also exploited this source). The same areas were also sources of hippopotamus ivory, since the animals existed in the Nile Delta and the Orontes Valley. During the 13th century increasing turmoil in these areas surely had an impact on the availability of ivory. Certainly there is little sign that ivory carving persisted in the Aegean after the collapse of the palatial centres in LH IIIB2. It is likely that the decline began somewhat earlier, though when is impossible to say. Unfortunately the finds from the Citadel House Area give only tantalizing clues; firm proof is elusive.

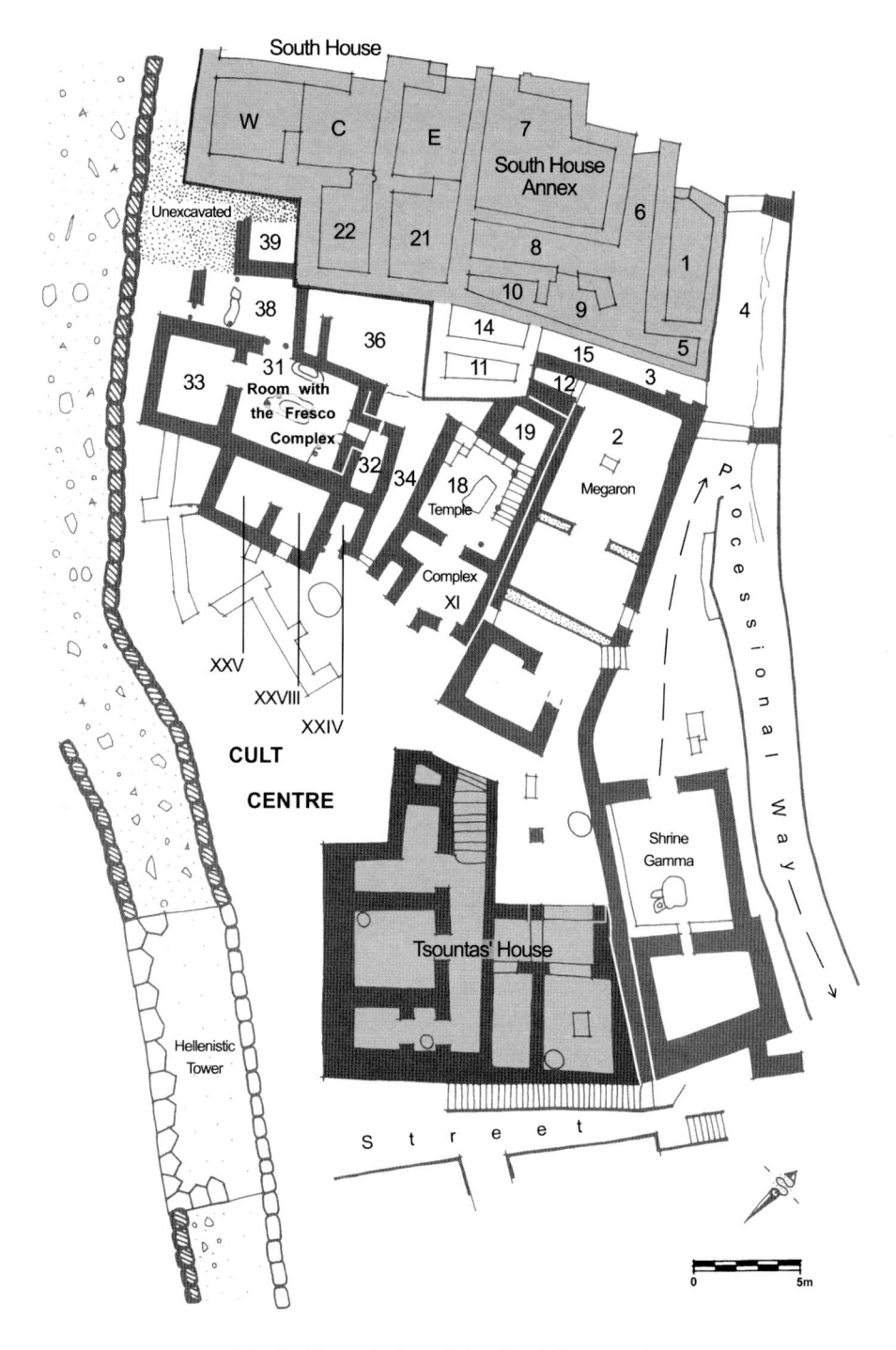

Fig. 1. General plan of the Citadel House Area.

FIND CONTEXTS AND CHRONOLOGY

Most of the ivories derive from LH IIIB contexts, specifically from phases VII and VIII in the site's history. All but a handful come from seven main areas. The deposits in Rooms II, 19, 31, 32, and 36 have been assigned to phase VII (catastrophe in the third quarter of the 13th century, often referred to as 'mid LH IIIB'). Room 18 and South House Annex Room 7 were destroyed at the end of LH IIIB2 (phase VIII). In addition a few ivories were recovered from LH IIIC levels (phases IX, X, XI), but they should be regarded as residual LH IIIB products. A single ivory object, inlay strip **I-35**, has been assigned to phase VI (terrace fill below LH IIIB structures). None was recovered from phase XIV (Hellenistic) levels. The distribution of bone, antler and boar's tusk differs somewhat and will be set out in Part 2, although the more important objects in these materials are mentioned here for sake of completeness. Complete lists, by context, appear on pp. 477–83. Fig. 1 provides a general plan of the Citadel House Area and adjacent structures. Detailed plans for phases VII, XI and XII can be found on pp. 490–91.

PHASE VII (CATASTROPHE IN THE COURSE OF LH IIIB)

The finds from two areas — Rooms II and 32 — are very similar in character (Figs. 4–5). Both contained items which are ostensibly finished, but probably not in use, as well as various kinds of partly worked ivory (see below, Room II). Similar pieces came from Area 36 and a few strays were also found in Room 31 and further afield. Further analysis of this 'workshop material' appears below (p. 36 ff; see also Krzyszkowska 1992*a*; 1997). These finds contrast markedly with a few other ivories, which were clearly finished and in use at the time of the catastrophe. These include the male head (**I-1**), lion (**I-2**) and pommel (**I-17**) from Room 31 and the ivories found with other objects in Room 19.

Room II

This, together with Room I, forms part of the basement of the Megaron, which is located on the upper terrace. The function of the building is uncertain, since few finds were recovered from ground-floor levels (*WBM* 1, 18–19, 33; French 1981, 44–5). Although the Megaron, like the Temple, remained in use until the phase VIII destruction, the ivories from the basement room(s) are assumed to belong to phase VII (the area is still under study). Room II contained numerous inlays (e.g. **I-30**, **I-31**, **I-37**, **I-41** to **I-43**, **I-45**, **I-46**, **I-49**; fragments **I-55** to **I-57**), but there is reason to doubt that any were in use at the time of the catastrophe. Some strips certainly seem to require additional work, e.g. trimming or polishing. Even the rosettes and lilies (**I-42**, **I-43**, **I-45**, **I-46**) could be construed as left-overs from larger job-lots. **I-22** may have been intended as a knife handle; perhaps it was damaged and retained as salvage. There are some unfinished pieces (e.g. **I-60**, perhaps abandoned during the course of manufacture) and several blanks (**I-66**, **I-67**). Fig. 4 provides a convenient overview of the principal pieces (cf. Krzyszkowska 1992*a*, 146, pl. LVII). Also found were a large unworked segment of hippopotamus lower canine (**I-84**; Pl. 16) and a quantity of unworked boar's tusk (**BT-8** to **BT-14**). From a disturbed area (context 0829) over Room II came a few inlay fragments (**I-32**, **I-44**, **I-47**), a waste segment (**I-78**), a bone pin (**B-35**) and a marble pommel (*WBM* 27, 23 no. 41). All should probably be associated with the material found in Room II.

Room 19

The Temple Complex, comprising Rooms 18, 19 and a small alcove, is situated on a second terrace, about 5.5 m below the Megaron. Room 19 — a small space reached by a flight of steps from Room 18 — contained a deposit of terracotta snakes and large anthropomorphic figures (*WBM* 1, 10, 18, 47–8; *WBM* 10, 17, 46–71). It was deliberately sealed following the phase VII catastrophe, whereas Room 18 was re-used during Phase VIII (see below). In Room 19 a few small ivories (Fig. 2) were found inside a small unpainted bowl, along with numerous beads made of glass, amber and semi-precious stones (*WBM* 10, 18–19, fig. 5). The ivories were probably offerings, whether dedicated individually or as a group is impossible to determine. The comb (**I-4**) is a small example of a common Mycenaean type, while the cosmetic implement (**I-9**, Pl. 5), though unusual, is not entirely unparalleled in the LBA Aegean. By contrast the small figurine (**I-3**, Pl. 5) has a rather foreign look about it, but its origins are hard to determine. If imported, it was not alone as the bowl also contained a scarab of Queen Tiye (*WBM* 10, 18–19, 113, fig. 5). Among the beads is one possible example in ivory (**I?-11**). Also found in Room 19 were a conulus or button (**I-12**) and a possible box-lid and peg (**I-10**). The Temple Complex is alone among the main phase VII structures in *not* yielding ivory 'workshop material'.

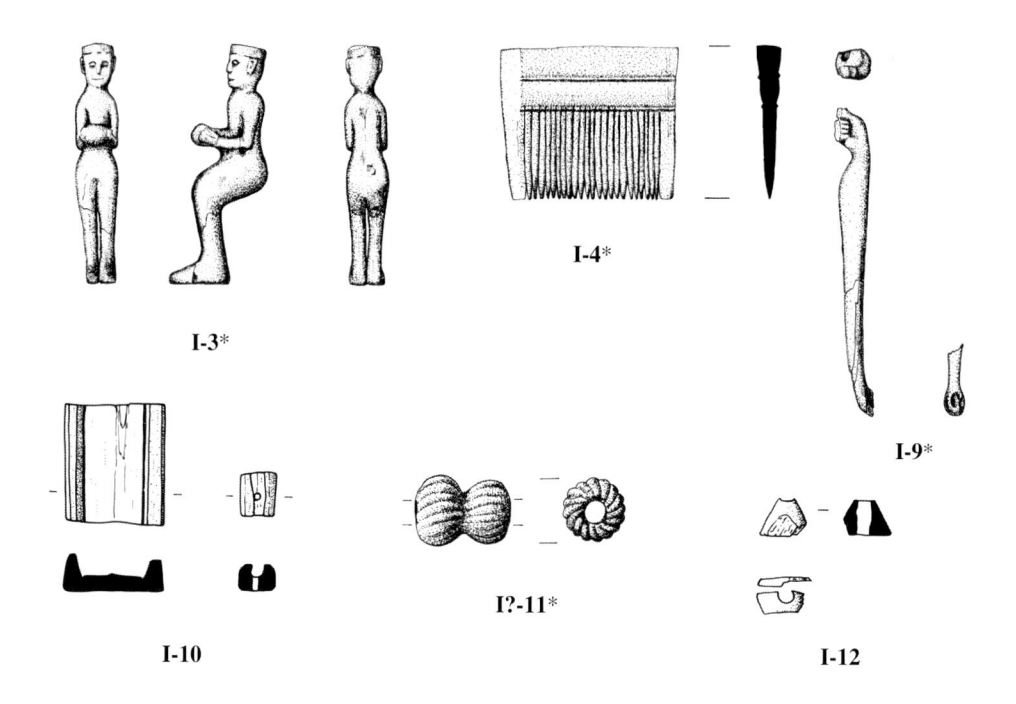

Fig. 2. Ivories from Room 19 (those found in bowl marked *). Phase VII.
Scale: **I-?11** 1:1, all others 1:2.

Room 31
Another cult area, The Room with the Fresco Complex (Rooms 31, 32, 33, 38), lies to the W of the Temple Complex. The two finest ivories from the site were discovered in Room 31, which also possessed an altar and elliptical hearth, in addition to the fresco from which the room takes its name (*WBM* 1, 48–9, 52; *Ant.* 1970, 174–7). The room also contained a clay larnax, a vat of unbaked clay, drinking vessels, storage and cooking jars (French 1999, 191). Inside a large lead vessel was found part of a faience plaque of Amenophis III (Cline 1995, 100, no. 25, pl. 6,3). Several outstanding finds came to light at the southern end of the altar. One was the magnificent lion (**I-2**, Pls. 3–4), carved substantially in the round, but provided with a mortise on the underside for attachment to a base or stand. Here too was a large ivory pommel (**I-17**, Fig. 3, Pl. 6) and a Minoan bird's-nest bowl of serpentine (*WBM* 27, 6–7 no. 3, fig. 1). The remarkable male head (**I-1**, Pls. 1–2) was recovered nearby, apparently fallen from the altar. The head, lion and pommel were certainly in use in the room prior to the phase VII catastrophe, though their precise function requires careful evaluation (see discussion pp. 21–5). A small piece of waste or scrap ivory (**I-80**) found near the head is probably best seen as a stray from the main group of 'workshop material' in Room 32 (below). The same may also be true of a

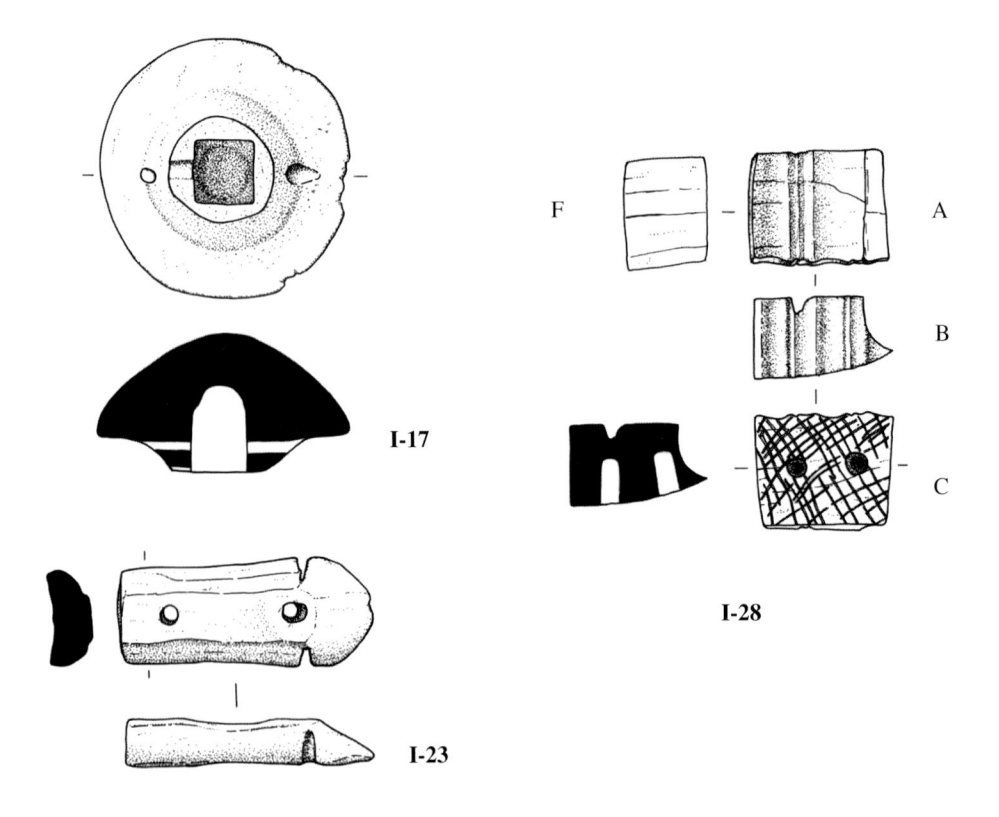

Fig. 3. Ivories from Room 31. Phase VII. Scale 1:2. For head **I-1** and lion **I-2** see Pls. 1–4.

solitary *pièce de lyre* (**I-23**), which may have been saved as salvage. Other likely strays from Room 32 are an unusual moulding (**I-28**, Fig. 3, Pl. 7) and an antler tool (**A-5**), found in the infill following the phase VII catastrophe. Following this event Rooms 31 and 32 were filled and went out of use, but the area was completely covered in the great destructions at the end of phase VIII (LH IIIB2). Material may also have been dispersed during building of the terraces at the beginning of phase IX. These facts may help to account for the scatter of finished and partly worked ivories in the general vicinity of Rooms 31, 32 and 36 which were associated with early LH IIIC material (see phase IX below). Most, if not all, probably belong with the phase VII deposit of ivories associated with Room 32.

Room 32

This small room, evidently a storeroom-cum-shrine, forms part of the Room with the Fresco Complex (*WBM* 1, 17, 49, 52). Indeed a doorway adjacent to the altar and fresco in Room 31 provides the only access to Room 32 (despite a narrow gap in the N wall). A terracotta wheel-made figure with upraised arms was found in the SW corner (*Ant.* 1970, pl. 42). Most of the ivories came from the N side of the room, near the doorway; all have been assigned to the phase VII floor deposit. The assemblage here is comparable to that found in Room II (Fig. 5 illustrates the principal pieces; cf. Krzyszkowska 1992*a*, 147, pl. LVIII). Noteworthy are the Naue II hilt-plates (**I-20**, **I-21**, Pl. 6) and knob (**I-19**), which should be regarded as salvage. Also found were two inlay strips, one perhaps unfinished (**I-33**, **I-34**), and a damaged spoon (**I-8**, Pl. 5). Remarkable is the quantity of partly worked ivory, including unfinished items (**I-61**, **I-62**), a blank (**I-68**), and irregular off-cuts (**I-72** to **I-76**). Especially important is a large cube, now badly decayed (**I-70**; Pl. 13). A worked horn core (**H-1**, Fig. 11, Pl. 19) and two antler tools (**A-3**, **A-4**, Fig. 11) were also found here. The latter compare well to those found in Area 36. As already noted, a few stray ivories, possibly originating in Room 32, were found overlying Room 31 and with Early LH IIIC material in Rooms 33, 38, xxiv and xxviii (below p. 14).

Area 36

This is an open area situated N of the Room with the Fresco complex, which was provisionally designated the 'Workshop' during the excavations (*WBM* 1, 9, 17–18, 40). An important find from this area was a steatite mould for jewellery (*WBM* 27, 29 no. 49, pl. 4). The ivories (see Fig. 6) should probably be associated with the phase VII catastrophe. Whether they are all in primary context is another matter, since most were found slightly above 'Floor 2'. The same also applies to a fine bronze awl with bone handle (**B-3**), a bone needle (**B-27**) and an antler tool (**A-10**). Other tools (**B-57**, **A-6** to **A-9**) are associated with the phase VII floor, so too is **I-38**, a broken (but finished?) inlay strip. The ivories found include two fragmentary inlay strips, not necessarily finished and in use (**I-39**, **I-40**); two unfinished items, perhaps damaged during manufacture (**I-63**, **I-64**); and a waste segment (**I-77**). Thus the range of material is comparable to that found in nearby Room 32 and also Room II. The complete absence of *débitage* (chips, trimmings and small off-cuts) indicates that Area 36 was not the site of an ivory workshop. A small T-shaped inlay (**I-50**, Fig. 8) and a small piece of scrap (**I-82**, Fig. 8) come from phase IX levels but should probably be seen as strays from LH IIIB. It is most likely that the stray pieces mentioned above were stored in Area 36 at the time of the catastrophe, as the infill from here was clearly moved in Phase IX.

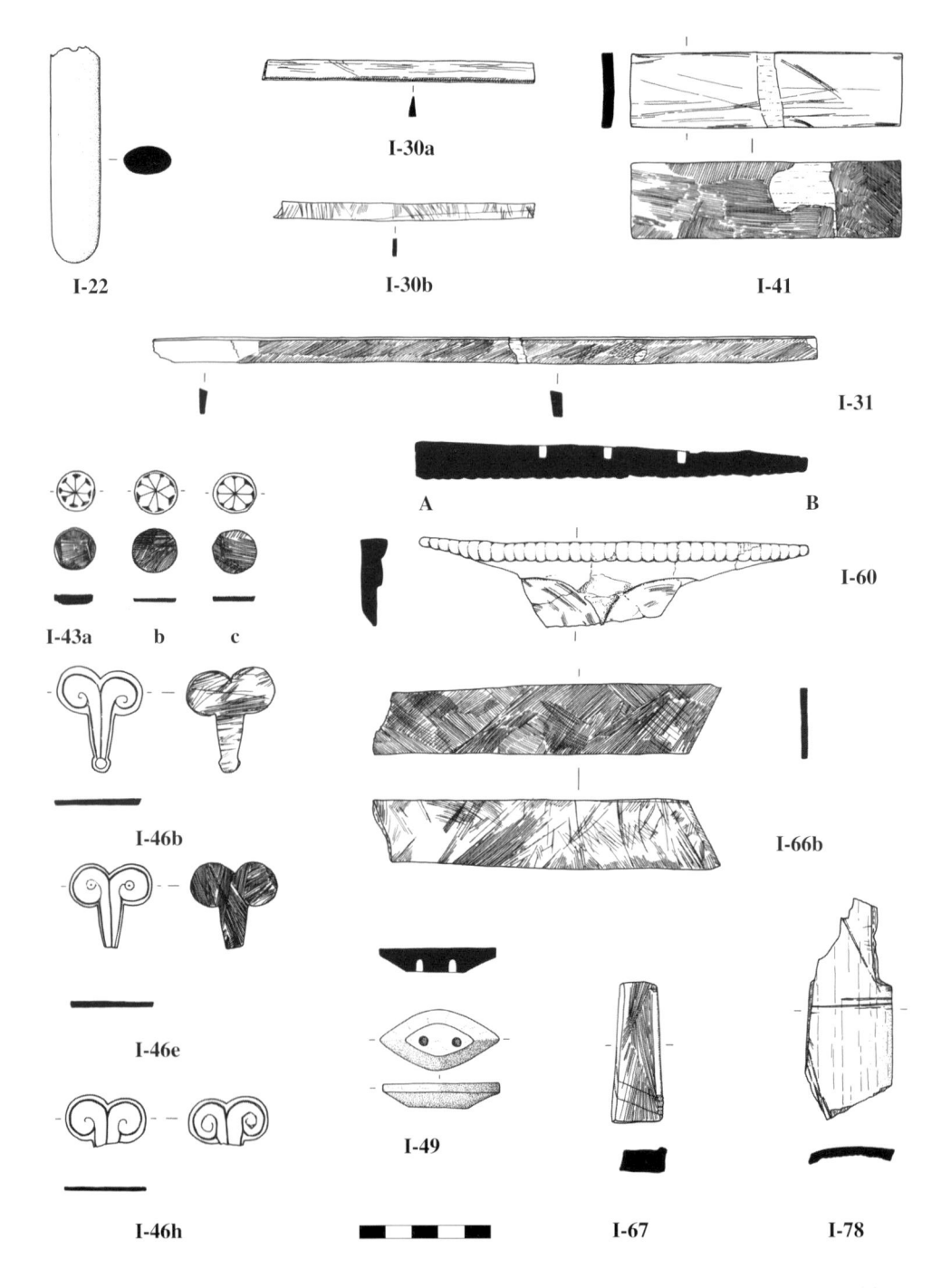

Fig. 4. Principal ivories from Room II. Phase VII. **I-78** found over Room II (context 0829). For hippopotamus tusk **I-84** see Pl. 16.

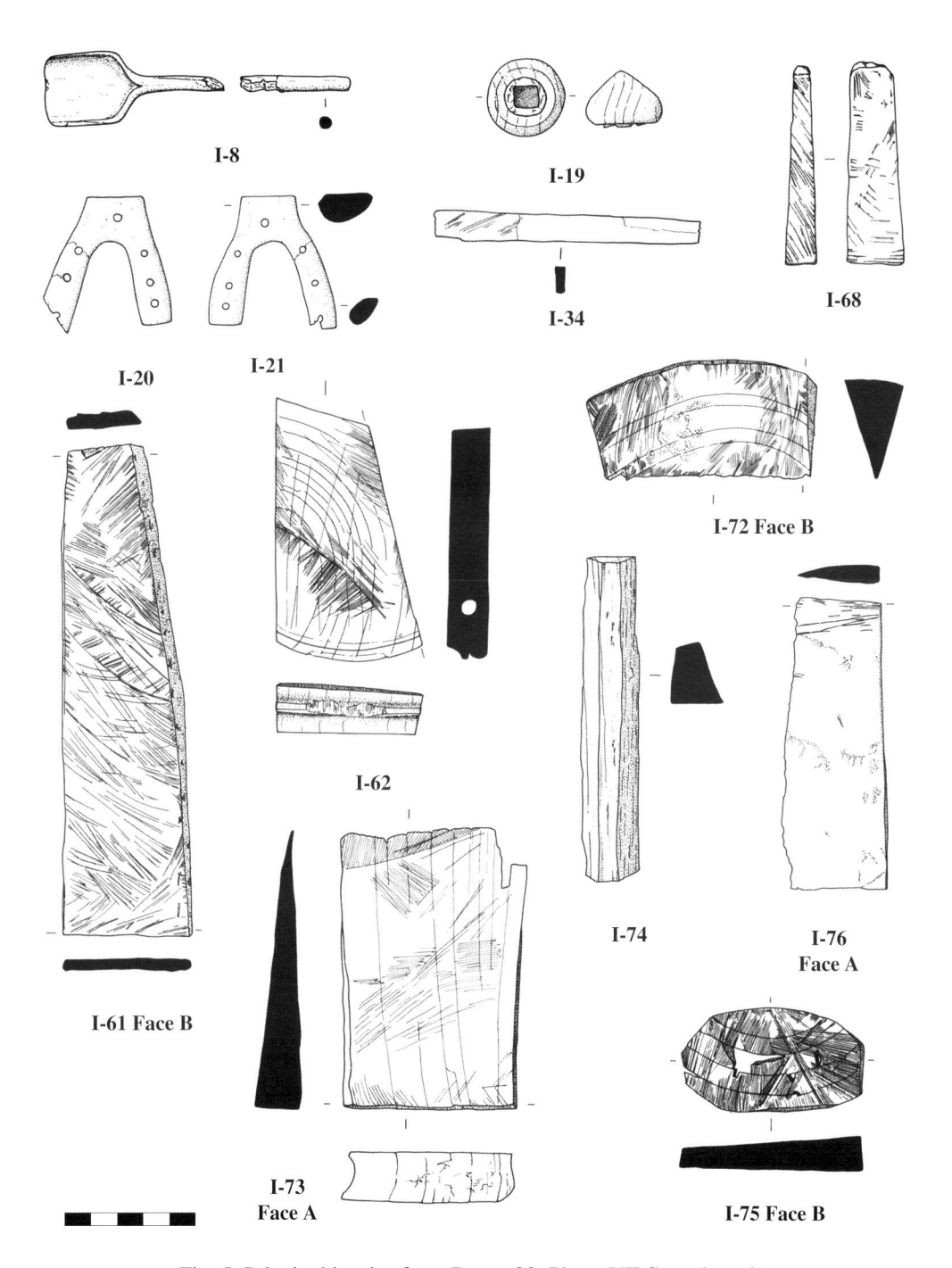

Fig. 5. Principal ivories from Room 32. Phase VII floor deposit.
For ivory cube **I-70** see Pl. 13.

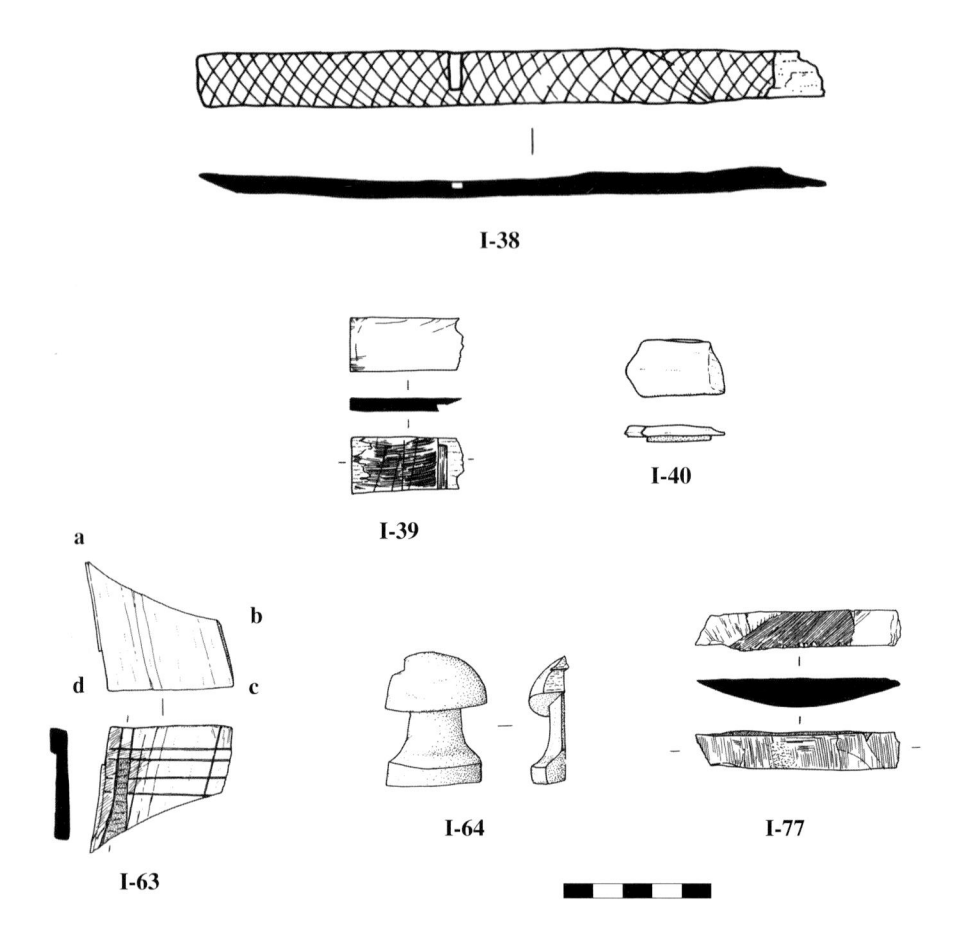

Fig. 6. Ivories from Area 36. **I-38** from Phase VII floor 2; remainder found above floor 2.

PHASE VIII (DESTRUCTION AT THE END OF LH IIIB2)

Unlike the phase VII ivories, those found in phase VIII contexts are rather disappointing and, in some cases, too fragmentary to understand. They were found in the fill of Room 18 of the Temple Complex and Room 7 in the South House Annex. Several important pieces were also discovered in destruction debris associated with the Causeway Deposit (*BSA* 68, 297–342; 339–40). However, the scarcity of objects from the Phase VIII destruction, in contrast to the prolific finds of Phase VII, was a feature throughout the area.

Room 18

This room continued in use until the major destruction which marked the end of phase VIII (*WBM* 1, 18, 47–8; *WBM* 10, 30–1). However, there are very few finds in ivory and related materials. A fine bone needle (**B-26**) was discovered below the upper floor and thus should belong to phase VII use. From the phase VIII upper fill and wash levels come two items: a ribbed appliqué (**I-27**, Fig. 7) and a tool (**B-59**). Finally, on the floor of the alcove behind Room 18

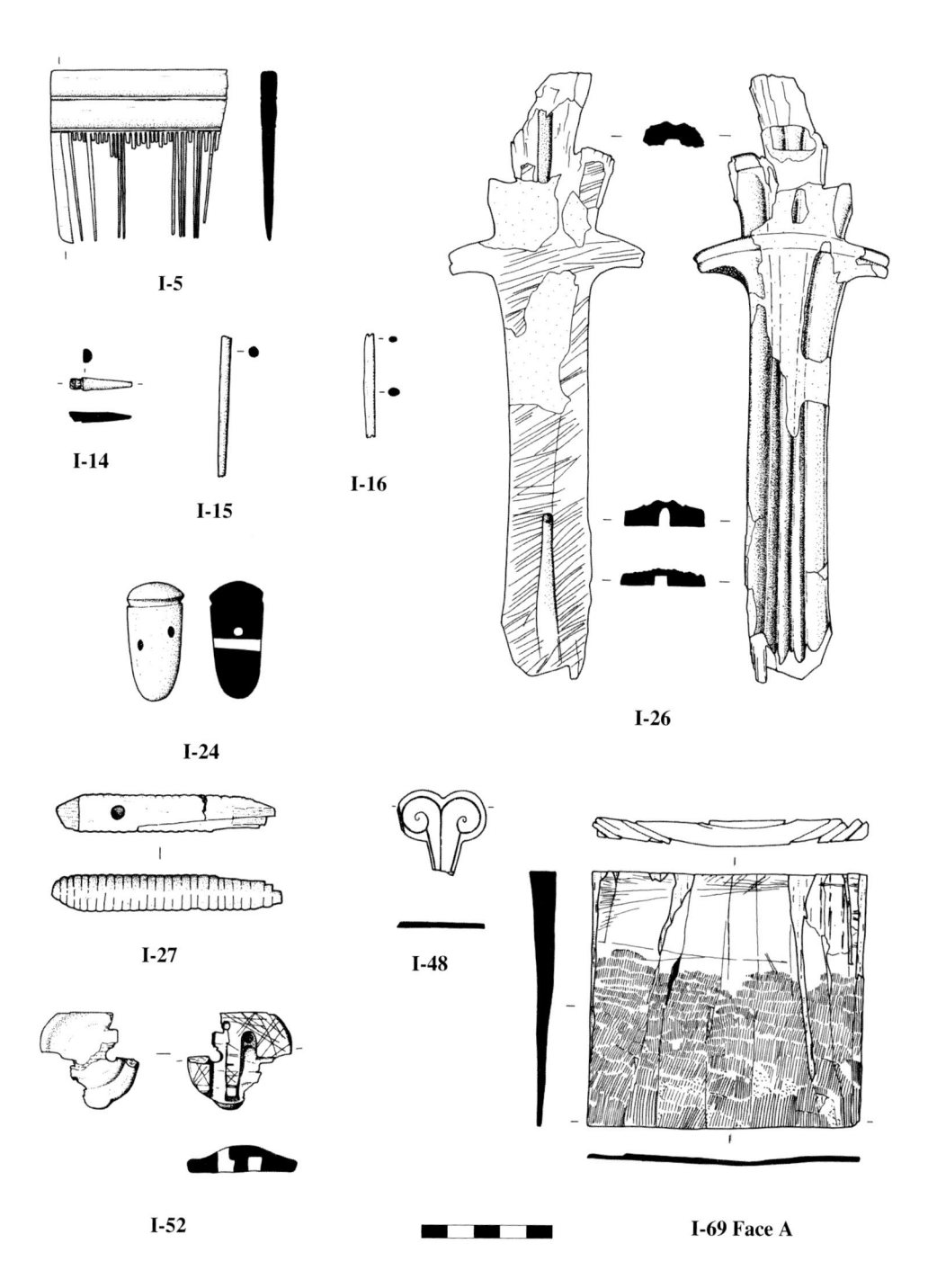

Fig. 7. Selected ivories from Phase VIII deposits. See also figure-of-eight toggle **I-13** (Pl. 5), pommel **I-18** (Pl. 6) and indeterminate objects **I-53** and **I-54** (Pl. 9).

was found a partly worked antler tine (**A-17**), which must also be originally associated with Phase VII.

Room 7 (South House Annex)
This room forms part of a complex which lies N of the Megaron and E of the South House itself. Room 7 seems to have been one of the principal rooms in the Annex, a room of some importance. It continued in use during phase VIII and was destroyed in the major LH IIIB2 destruction (*WBM* 1, 9–10, 16, 30). The ivories recovered here all seem to represent articles in use at the time of the destruction (Fig. 7 illustrates a selection). However, all are badly burnt, sometimes beyond recognition. This is certainly true of a large quadrangular slab (**I-53**, Pl. 9), just possibly part of a box. It belongs to the phase VIII floor deposit, as does a badly deformed appliqué (**I-52**). Another enigmatic appliqué (**I-26**, Pl. 7), apparently representing a dagger, comes from the collapse associated with the phase VIII destruction. Also found were a bronze knife with bone (or possibly ivory) handle, now badly damaged (**B/I-1**, Fig. 12) and a fragmentary pin (**I-15**). In the upper fill was found an 'acorn-shaped object', probably a stopper (**I-24**), and part of a toggle (**I-14**). Both conform closely to known Mycenaean types; neither shows signs of burning.

Causeway Deposit and associated areas (*BSA* 68, 297–342)
At the NE end of the site, part of a well-laid poros ramp or causeway was uncovered, leading from the vicinity of the Ramp House to Corridor 4. A deposit of LH IIIB2 pottery was found here, fallen from above in the course of the final destruction. This was covered with a mass of rubble, burnt mud-brick and calcined debris. Four ivories were found in this area (*BSA* 68, 339–40, fig. 23, pl. 61). A fine but badly burnt sword pommel (**I-18**, Pl. 6) came to light outside the entrance to Room 6, just above floor level. The pendant or toggle in the shape of a figure-of-eight shield (**I-13**, Pl. 5) was recovered from destruction debris over the causeway and thus possibly had fallen from above. Two more pieces came from near the entrance to Room 1 (a storeroom containing large jars: *WBM* 1, 16–17; *BSA* 68, 301). One is a puzzling piece with moulding (**I-54**, Pl. 9), apparently belonging to a finished object. The other, a blank for a comb (**I-69**, Fig. 7, Pl. 12), is the only 'workshop material' from the phase VIII destruction. It is unfortunate that the context is not more informative.

Three more ivories were found in Phase VIII destruction debris (Fig. 7). One is a small comb of standard Mycenaean type (**I-5**) found in the North Courtyard, not far from the Causeway. In addition there is a fragment of a lily inlay (**I-48**) from Room 2, the Megaron; and a fragmentary needle (**I-16**) from the floor of the Small Courtyard at the south.

PHASE IX (EARLY LH IIIC)
Eleven ivories came from phase IX contexts (Fig. 8). As mentioned above, most are probably strays from the main phase VII deposits, perhaps disturbed during the course of phase VIII or displaced in levelling at the beginning of Phase IX. The distribution bears this out — most come from the general vicinity of the Room with the Fresco complex — and there is certainly no reason to regard any as a LH IIIC product. The finds are as follows: a small wedge (**I-65**) from over Room 31; an oval attachment (**I-29**) and tusk tip (**I-71**) from levelling up in Room 33 and a damaged comb (**I-6**) from below Room xxxii. Among the debris in Room xxiv was an

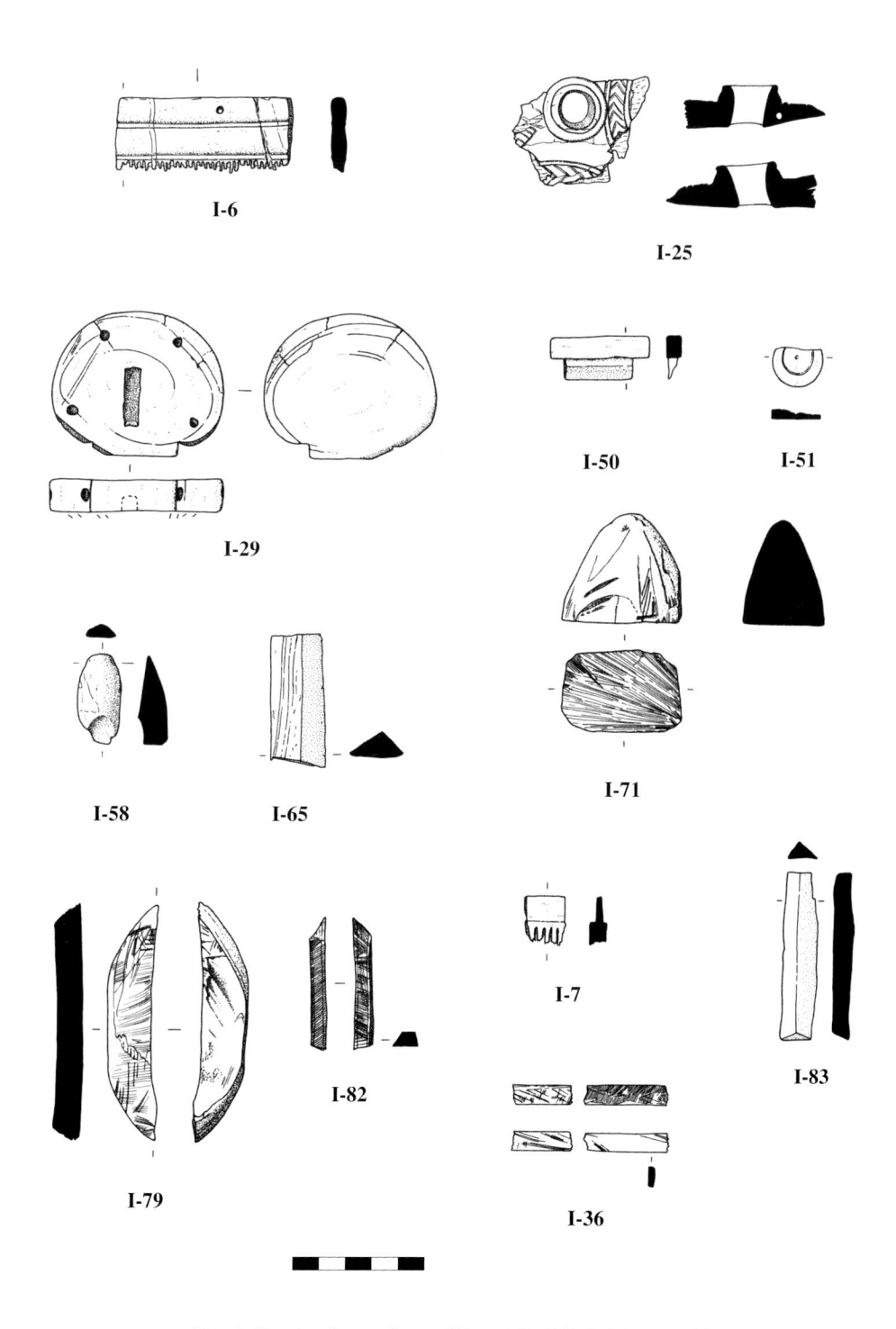

Fig. 8. Ivories from phases IX and X (**I-7**, **I-36** and **I-83**).

indeterminate fragment (**I-58**) and a small off-cut (**I-81**). In addition, two pieces came from Room xxxiv over Area 36: a small piece of scrap (**I-82**) and a T-shaped inlay (**I-50**). A broken disc inlay (**I-51**) was found among the debris in Enclosure cd/cc and a partly worked segment (**I-79**) came from the floor in Room xxxiii. Part of a so-called 'candlestick' (**I-25**) came from disturbed levels in the S scarp.

PHASE X (EARLY–TOWER PHASES OF LH IIIC)
By this phase even strays are a rarity. Three pieces — a tiny comb fragment (**I-7**), an inlay strip (**I-36**) and a small waste segment (**I-83**) — came from the upper fill of Rooms xxviii/xxiv.

PHASE XI (ADVANCED AND DEVELOPED PHASES OF LH IIIC)
No ivories are assigned to this phase or to later levels.

THE OBJECTS

Here discussion focuses on individual ivories and groups, generally following the catalogue order (pp. 103–285). Special attention is given to pieces which are unique or which add significantly to our understanding of Mycenaean ivories. General remarks concerning the different categories are found above (p. 3). It is, however, worth reiterating that these are intended as a broad framework only. Many pieces proved difficult to assign to specific categories; comments will be made as appropriate.

Carvings in the round
This technique is not well represented in the repertoire of Mycenaean ivories, which is essentially concerned with relief carving and inlay work. Apart from the *femme debout* figurines (Poursat 1977a, 49–51) there is no 'type' or style regularly to be found in three-dimensional carving. Most pieces which do exist are unique, a fact which impedes our ability to determine their origin. This is certainly true for the male head (**I-1**), lion (**I-2**) and small figurine (**I-3**).

The head of a young man (**I-1**, Pls. 1–2) — one of the most important ivories to survive from the LBA — has already received considerable attention, both in preliminary reports and in secondary literature. However, since most published comments have been brief (and some ill informed), a detailed discussion is presented here (with further details on pp. 104–5).

The head has been carved from a carefully selected section of elephant tusk, which preserves the natural tapering root cavity (Krzyszkowska 1988, 212, pls. 24 b–d). This feature, with little modification, runs vertically from the neck to the crown of the head (Pl. 2 *top*). The central hollow and four surviving holes on the circumference of the neck indicate that the head was designed for attachment to a central support or even to the neck and body of a wooden statuette. Just below the crown a small ledge or ridge was cut inside the hole, suggesting that an ivory disc had been inserted here to cover the hole and central support.

A substantial portion of the right-hand side of the neck is missing, but the head itself is relatively well preserved. Aside from small flakes missing from the fillet (and now a slightly larger segment from the chin) the only significant damage to the face occurs on the nose. The proportions of the head — broad at the temples and cheeks, tapering to a small rounded chin — emphasize the individual features. These are carefully executed and seem designed to convey a calm, yet compelling appearance. The large eyes are especially striking, consisting of discs within almond-shaped ridges, rendered in relief. There are no eyelashes (*pace* Demakopoulou 1988, 70). The eyebrows, also rendered in low relief, accentuate the eyes still further. The nose, though damaged, is fine and straight, but rather wedge-like. However, there is little modelling and the nostrils are merely indicated by short drill holes. The mouth is broad, but the actual lips are rather thin and compressed, producing a rather severe effect. The ears do not lie flat against the head, but protrude outwards. Both are drilled at the junction between upper and lower lobes. The position is somewhat curious for earrings, but attempting to pierce the fragile lower lobes would have been extremely risky. [Pierced ears are, of course, found on terracotta figures though not on those from the Cult Centre (Nicholls 1970, 4). Ed.]

Around the crown of the head is carved a plain band in low relief. It seems to sit very high on the head, especially in relation to the ears, perhaps representing a circlet of metal or some other sturdy material rather than a headband of cloth. Considerable effort has been given to rendering the hair. The mass of hair is set off from the head *per se* by a line of low relief, so that the head seems to wear a close-fitting wig. A central parting, aligned with the nose, occurs in the centre of the forehead. Individual strands of hair are rendered in an artificial manner, by a series of incised lines, which echo the hairline in the front, radiate outwards on the crown and run vertically from fillet to bottom edge at the back. A double relief ridge occurs at the lower edge of the neck, perhaps indicating the neckline of a garment.

There is some controversy over the origin of the head. Buchholz (*AA* 89 (1974), 436) asserted categorically — but without substantiating evidence — that it should be regarded as a Syrian work. Poursat (1977*a*, 53, 233) followed suit in considering the head an import and cited Near Eastern parallels for the treatment of certain details. However, Barnett, a leading authority on Near Eastern ivories, commented that the head did 'not strike [him] at all as a genuinely Oriental piece' (*JHS* 100 (1980), 286).

The main 'orientalizing' feature is the treatment of the hair on the forehead, which lacks good Aegean parallels. The central parting compares with a convention found on some Near Eastern carvings including the head of Ishtar from Mari, which is offered by Poursat as a close parallel (Poursat 1977*a*, 53, 233; *Syria* 17 (1936), 7–8). But in other respects the hair on the Ishtar is treated very differently. Of other eastern parallels cited by Poursat, the head of Baal from Ugarit is surely the least convincing. Even Poursat admits it to be 'très differente d'aspecte' (1977*a*, 53 n. 3). Indeed it is hard to see any resemblance to the Mycenae head, even in the most general terms. The Baal is made of ivory, but with extensive use of additional materials: gold, silver, copper, lapis lazuli and diorite (Safadi 1963; Barnett 1982, 29, pl. 23b). The use of lapis or other precious materials for inlaid eyebrows and pupils occurs in much Near Eastern work of bone, ivory and stone (e.g. the head of Ishtar above). Yet aside from the possible provision of earrings and perhaps gold on the headband, no precious materials could have been used on the Mycenae head. Finally, one may observe that most Near Eastern heads, including the Baal and Ishtar, have a rather fleshy appearance, with plump even bulging cheeks. This characteristic may also be seen in the 'mixed style' of Late Cypriot ivories (e.g. mirror handles and the Delos warrior plaque: Poursat 1977*a*, 159–60, pl. XVI; Krzyszkowska 1991, 116; 1992*b*, 240; Hood 1978,

PLATE 1

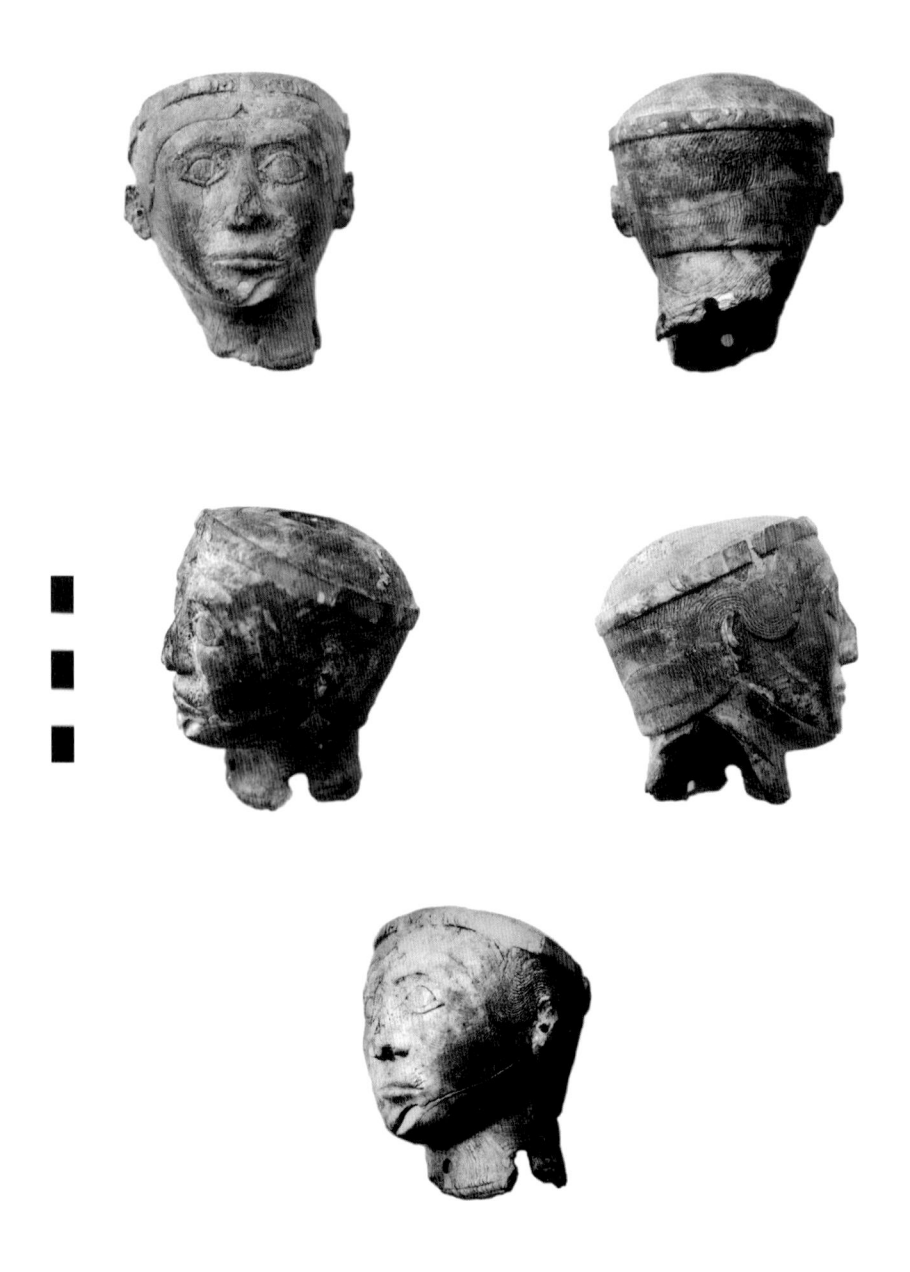

Ivory head **I-1**. Scale 1:2.

Ivory head **I-1**. Scale *top c.* 1:2, *bottom* 1:2.

fig. 121 for Delos plaque). The bronze horned god from Enkomi has similar features (Catling 1964, 255–6, pl. 46).

Heads rendered in the round are exceptional in the LBA Aegean. A small plaster head, found by Wace at Mycenae, has a vertical hole in the neck for attachment (*JHS* 59 (1939), 210 fig. 1). So too does the large plaster head, thought to be a sphinx, discovered by Tsountas (*AE* 1902, 1ff, pl. 1–2; Hood 1978, 102). If we make allowances for the differences in material and scale, the Tsountas head offers especially useful comparisons. The head is wide at the temples and cheeks and tapers sharply to a small rounded chin. The eyes are wide and set high in the face. They are rendered as solid black discs within almond-shaped outlines and are accentuated by long arching eyebrows. The nose is long and wedge-like. The lips are compressed: the upper is thin, the lower broader and curving. The red fillet (or edge of the cap) is set high on the head. On the temples, the hair loops down in front of the ear. The only significant differences are the 'hooks' of hair across the forehead and modelling around nose and mouth. The terracotta head from the LH IIIC shrine at Asine also provides parallels (*Asine* I, 74–6, 308 no. 1, figs. 206, 211). Here the vertical hole runs from the neck to the top of the head. The round bulging eyes (feasible in clay, but more difficult in ivory) are accentuated by arching eyebrows rendered as raised (i.e. relief) ridges. Although the ears hug the head (i.e. unlike those on **I-1**), they are provided with holes between the upper and lower lobes (side view in Demakopoulou 1988, cat. no. 24). These three Mycenaean heads are all much closer in appearance to **I-1** than any of the Near Eastern 'comparanda'.

Moreover, even among Mycenaean ivories there exist good parallels for the treatment of details. For instance, the use of the relief ridge to surround the eyeball (regarded by Poursat as an eastern feature) occurs on warrior head appliqués (Krzyszkowska 1991). Indeed on the best-preserved example from ChT 27 (NM 2468) the eyebrow is rendered as an arching ridge in very low relief (Xénaki-Sakellariou 1985, 98, pl. 22; Demakopoulou 1988, 236, cat. no. 238 colour). Another parallel is provided by a female figure from Mycenae (Poursat 1977*b*, cat. no. 335; Sakellarakis 1979, fig. 64 provides better illustration). Here the eye is an almond-shaped ridge surrounding a slightly bulging circular eyeball.

By far the closest parallel for this treatment of the eyes has so far passed unnoticed. It occurs on the preserved eye of the lion (**I-2**) found with the head in Room 31. The rendering of the eye is precisely the same on both; their size is comparable. There is little doubt that these two ivories have the same origin.

The couchant lion (**I-2**, Pls. 3–4) is one of the largest ivories yet recovered from a Mycenaean site. Unlike the head it has been carved from a solid section of tusk with no trace of the root cavity. The lion seems to have been carved wholly in the round, although into its underside is cut a long rectangular mortise. It is possible that this represents later re-working (below). However, the lion is not in good condition and this severely hampers our ability to assess technical details. Happily, though, the main features can still be appreciated. In the following description and in the catalogue, left and right relate to the *lion's* left side and right side.

The carving skilfully captures the latent power of a lion, with strongly modelled hindquarters, powerful shoulders and forelimbs, deeply articulated paws. There is no sign of stiffness or rigidity. The lion is depicted with its muzzle resting on its front paws. Though much of the face is lost to decay, the frontal view is still striking. The nose is wedge-shaped and flares to broad nostrils, indicated by deep triangular drillings. Only the left eye is preserved, but this is rendered in low relief as an almond-shaped ridge surrounding a flat disc. In shape and execution it offers close parallels for the eyes on the male head (**I-1**). Behind the eye, a modelled ruff marks the forward extent of the mane, which is rendered as a series of wavy feather-like incisions, stretching back as far as the shoulder in places. The traces are very faint indeed. Likewise vestigial is the left ear set high on the head near the ruff. The carved surface is wholly lost, leaving only a heart-shaped 'ghost' and fugitive remains of drillings. Virtually no trace of the right ear survives. Only a small segment of the tail remains, on the right flank of the lion.

The preservation on the underside is fractionally better, especially on the toes and forelimbs. Particularly striking is the powerful modelling and the well-articulated joints, indicated by relief ridges (Pl. 4). By contrast, the mortise seems crudely gouged — just missing the limbs — front and back. The edges are irregular and the depth somewhat uneven: in places it barely misses piercing through to the upper surface of the body. Can this really be an original feature? It certainly squares badly with the exceptionally fine carving seen elsewhere on the lion.

In Mycenaean ivory carving there is no uniform convention for depicting lions, whether in terms of pose or in the treatment of details. Lions carved wholly or substantially in the round are virtually non-existent. The couchant lion which serves as a handle on the Agora pyxis provides a distant parallel, but the scale is very much smaller and the function entirely different (*Agora* XIII, B1 511, pl. 32). Moreover, the head is turned, whereas ours faces forwards. Most representations of lions are executed in low relief (e.g. on plaques or combs) and they are normally shown attacking another animal, e.g. a bull (Poursat 1977a, 68–9 list). One convention, which is more or less constant in all cases, is the feather-like treatment of the mane.

Although specific parallels are hard to find, there is certainly nothing un-Mycenaean about our lion. Poursat remarks that its large size makes it 'une pièce exceptionnelle', but does not question its origin (1977a, 69, 71, pl. III). Unfortunately, he was unaware that one eye was preserved, thus providing a conclusive link to the head (pers. comm.).

Unique pieces are inherently difficult to interpret — the head and lion are no exceptions. Moreover, style and technique aside, their function needs careful evaluation. Both pieces were found in the Room with the Fresco, one of several cult areas or shrines situated on the south-west slope. The lion was found at the southern end of the altar, on the altar, along with pommel **I-17** (below p. 29) and the Minoan stone bowl; the head had fallen to the ground nearby to the west. In other words, the objects may well have been *on display* in the room at the time of the phase VII catastrophe. But was their use in the room primary or secondary? And what exactly was their purpose or meaning? For each object we are confronted with several possibilities:

i. The use of the head in the Room is primary, i.e. it had been specially commissioned for the shrine. If so, attached to its support or wooden body, the head could be interpreted as follows:
   a. It was an anthropomorphic representation of the deity, serving as a cult image, i.e. the object of veneration within the shrine (or indeed outside, if carried there).
   b. It was an anthropomorphic representation of a deity, serving as a votive offering within the shrine.
   c. It represented an attendant or votary and served as a votive offering within the shrine.
ii. The use of the lion in the Room is likewise primary, i.e. specially commissioned for the shrine. If so, it could be interpreted as follows:
   a. It was explicitly designed as a companion piece for the head, with symbolic meaning, e.g. for a Master of Animals tableau.
   b. It served as a votive offering and had been made for that purpose.

PLATE 3

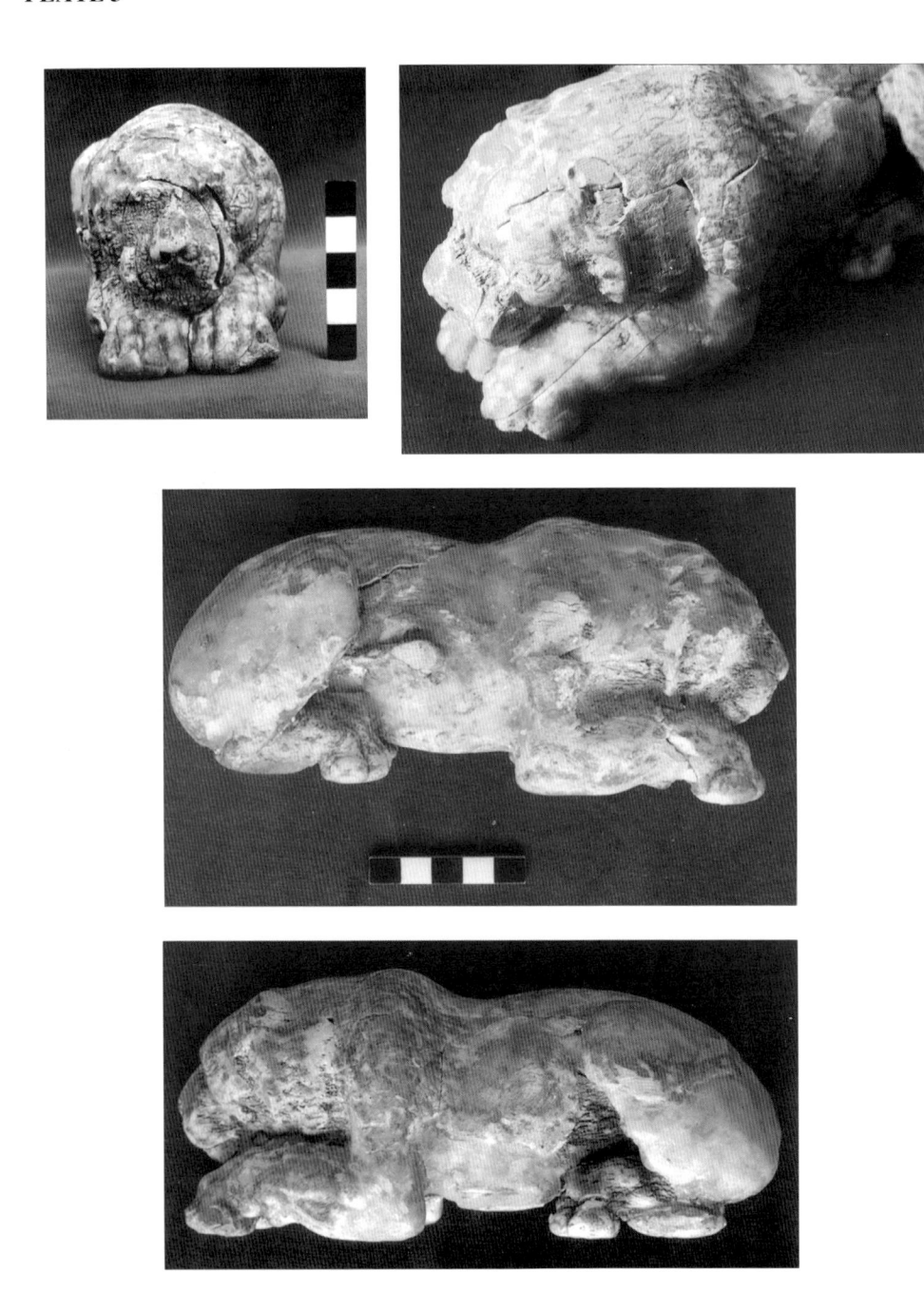

Ivory lion **I-2**. Scale: *top left, centre* and *bottom* 1:2; *top right* not to scale.

PLATE 4

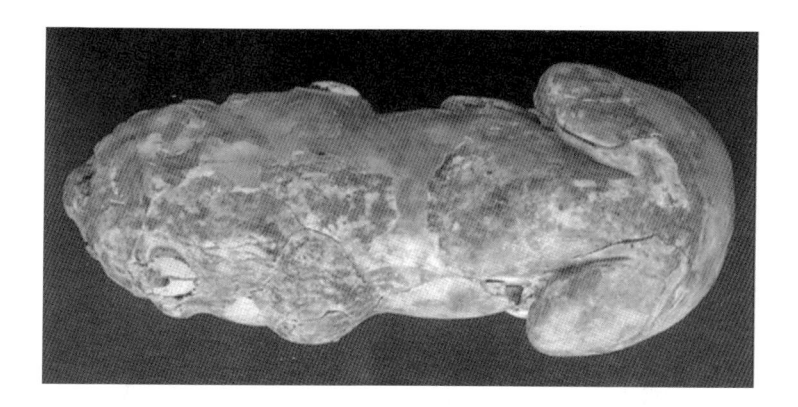

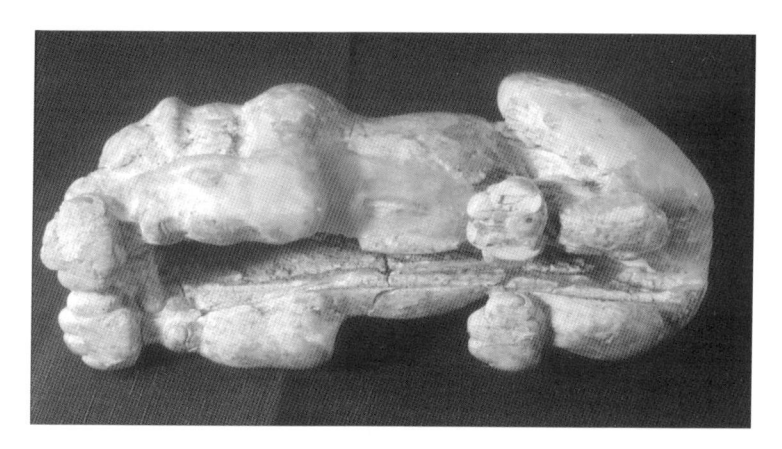

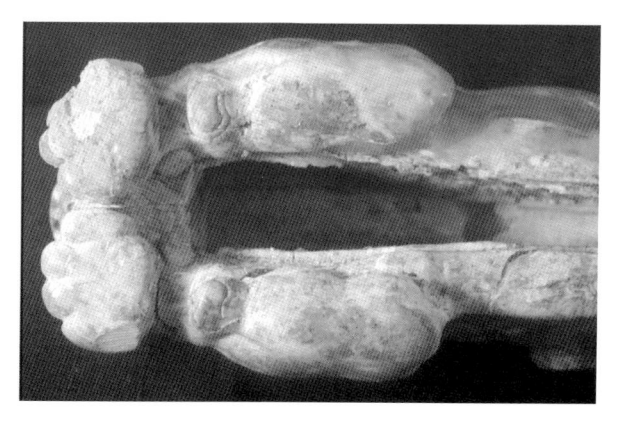

Ivory lion **I-2**. Scale: *top* and *centre c*. 1:2; *bottom* not to scale.

iii. The use of the head and the lion in the Room is secondary. This too, fails to provide unequivocal answers regarding their purpose and meaning. Once displayed in the Room the pieces may have retained their original meaning(s) or they may have acquired new ones.

The head, made of an imported material, attached to a stand or wooden body, would have made an impressive sight, standing perhaps half a metre high. This is comparable to some of the Type B figures in the Temple Complex or indeed to the very much earlier chryselephantine figure from LM IB Palaikastro (MacGillivray *et al.* 2000). But neither size nor striking appearance completely solves the question of function. The Type B figures are more likely to be votives or attendant votaries than representations of deities, because we are dealing with a series of images (*WBM* 10, 100–1). And while the Palaikastro figure has been hailed as representing the youthful Minoan divinity, proof positive is lacking — not least because the figure was not in a primary context. We face much the same dilemma with almost every anthropomorphic figure in the Aegean Bronze Age, from early Cretan vessel-figures to the so-called Goddesses with Uplifted Arms. In the Mycenaean world, the Type A female figures present similar difficulties, as does the large male figure from Phylakopi (Renfrew 1985, 372–3). Not only is our male figure unique, the loss of the wooden body deprives us of evidence for gesture. However, it is worth stressing that this was the sole three-dimensional anthropomorphic image in the room and was probably displayed in a prominent location. As such, it is certainly a good candidate for a cult image.

The exact status of the lion is also hard to establish. There is no way of proving it was made as a companion piece for the head. Though their eyes are undoubtedly similar, this merely points to a common convention and does not mean they emanated from the same workshop or were carved by the same hand. Thus to regard the lion as part of a Master of Animals tableau is probably stretching the evidence too far. However, the symbolic role of lions in Mycenaean iconography is well documented and, as a votive, this magnificent carving would have held particular resonance. That said, there is little evidence to show that ivories were produced *explicitly* for votive use in the LBA Aegean (cf. p. 26: **I-3**).

Indeed, we cannot exclude possibility that the use of the lion and head in the Room is secondary. Since the pieces lack comparanda, there is no means of dating them closely. In other words, they might be older than their context. Other items in the Room — notably the Minoan stone bowl and the faience plaque of Amenophis III (68-1000) — are undoubtedly heirlooms. Of course, re-use in the Room does not necessarily demand a change in function. It may be a case of once a cult image, always a cult image. However, much hangs on whether the head was indeed still attached to its wooden body or stand at the time of the catastrophe. This is hard to establish. The severe damage to the neck and the absence of non-joining fragments is a trifle worrisome. So too is the damage to the nose, which might be old (certainly it contrasts markedly with the fresh breaks on the chin and fillet). There is no trace of the disc (presumably ivory) which covered the hole in the top of the head (above p. 16). Unfortunately, these observations do not offer conclusive proof — one way or the other — regarding the state of the head immediately prior to the catastrophe. However, even disembodied, the head is a fine piece made from a valuable material and as such would have been a suitable offering to the shrine. The same holds good for the superb lion, whose clumsy mortise hints at earlier transformations, as well as the ivory pommel (**I-17**) detached from its sword (below p. 29).

The Room with the Fresco represents one of the most important cult areas to survive from the Aegean Bronze Age. Moreover, the catastrophe at the end of phase VII ensured that the room and contents survived without the complications of re-use which so often cloud our understanding of Aegean cult. It is, therefore, especially irritating that there are lingering doubts regarding the status of the head and lion prior to the catastrophe. The simplest explanation — that the head served as the cult image of this shrine complex — is undoubtedly the most attractive. We can only hope that future discoveries will bring corroboration.

Our third carving in the round (**I-3**) is a small figurine, which comes from the Temple Complex, another suite of rooms used for cult purposes. The piece represents a seated male figure, the pose rendered by bent hips and knees (Fig. 2, Pl. 5). The feet are large and flat. Curiously, there are no dowels for attachment to a seat or stool (see below). The arms are bent at the elbows and the hands appear to hold a small pear-shaped object. On his head, the figure seems to wear a flat cap or polos, marked by a line of incision. Given the small scale, facial features are rendered in a cursory manner.

As already noted, carvings in the round are not well represented in the repertoire of Mycenaean ivories. Male figurines are all but non-existent. Mycenae ChT 27 contained a small 'adorant', with wasp-waist, arm placed across chest, and wearing a kilt or loincloth (Poursat 1977*a*, 52–3; 1977*b*, cat. no. 286). A so-called *femme debout* figurine wearing a flounced skirt was found in the same tomb (Poursat 1977*a*, 49–59; 1977*b*, cat. no. 287). Both figurines are in very poor condition, so it is impossible to say whether they were intended as companion pieces (the male is decidedly smaller). In any case, typologically they go back to Minoan figurines, well documented in clay and bronze.

By contrast there are no convincing parallels in the Aegean for our figurine. However, seated figures made of bronze are attested in LBA Syro-Palestine and Cyprus. While none offers an especially close parallel, the general concept is undoubtedly similar. The Syro-Palestinian examples represent both male and female figures (rulers or divinities?) wearing long garments and tall 'Syrian' caps (e.g. Frankfort 1970, figs. 297–300, 322; also Seeden 1982, 111–18, nos. 11–23). Their arms are usually bent at the elbow, though gestures differ from one figure to the next. Indeed it would be wrong to speak of a common 'type', simply a common pose. Although some are close to our figure in size, others are significantly larger (i.e. up to 25 cms). Three bronzes from Enkomi may be distantly related. Two were found in Bâtiment 18, one still seated on an elaborate chair with a footstool; the third was a stray find (Catling 1964, 253–4, nos. 2–5, pl. 45).

Several important features set our figurine apart from the eastern examples: material, size, dress (or lack thereof) and head-dress. There are no dowels or other means of attachment to seat or support (although some bronzes lack this feature too). Clearly, in the absence of convincing parallels it is difficult to claim the Mycenae figure as an import, though it would be rash to exclude the possibility altogether. Perhaps we are dealing with an 'orientalizing' work, drawing on a conventional pose common in the East, combined with Aegean features (absence of a robe, presence of a polos). While this explanation is not altogether satisfactory, it serves to reinforce the dilemmas posed by unique pieces.

Happily the function of this modest figurine — unlike the imposing ivory head — is easy enough to interpret. It was found in a bowl containing numerous beads of glass and semi-precious materials (carnelian, rock crystal, amber, lapis lazuli), as well as other exotica, e.g. the faience scarab of Queen Tiye (*WBM* 10, 18–19, 113, fig. 5). There is no doubt that the contents of the bowl were offerings, made to the Temple during phase VII and sealed in Room 19 following the upheaval in the middle of LH IIIB. Of course, the primary function of the figurine cannot be established. There is, however, scant evidence that ivories were produced explicitly as votives (or indeed as grave goods). When they do occur in sanctuaries (or burials) we are effectively dealing with secondary use (cf. Krzyszkowska 2003, 190–1: IvTir cat. no. 36).

Brief mention here may be made of the small broken figurine of the *femme debout* type found by Mylonas in T9 (*PAE* 1973, 101, pl. 124a; Poursat 1977*a*, 49, pl. III,8), which corresponds to Room 33 in the Helleno-British excavations. Thus perhaps this figurine should also be regarded as a stray from the main group of ivories found in Rooms 31 and 32 (above pp. 8–9). In any case, it may well have been a votive.

Cosmetic articles and jewellery

Among the finest Mycenaean ivory carvings are cosmetic articles — combs, pyxides and mirror handles — lavishly decorated in low relief (Poursat 1977*a*, 18–27). Though well represented in the chamber tombs at Mycenae, they are conspicuously absent on the acropolis. Nor were they to be found in the Houses of Shields and Sphinxes. Further afield the picture is much the same. However, archaeological chance may be the operative factor, since deliberate deposition in tombs favours the survival of ivories and other elite products. Unfortunately few tombs are closely datable and heirlooms can further cloud the picture. Another complicating factor is decline in rich burials during LH IIIA2–B, as more resources were channelled into palatial construction and, perhaps, as access to prestige goods became ever more restricted (Voutsaki 2000). Unfortunately, the few cosmetic items from the Citadel House Area shed no further light on this question. Aside from combs, this category includes a miscellany of small finds loosely associated with cosmetic purposes or personal adornment.

Three of our combs (**I-4**, **I-5**, **I-6**) belong to the standard Mycenaean type, widely attested during LH II–IIIB and characterized by a rectangular 'back' or handle provided with two plain horizontal ribs on each side. One rib usually occurs at roughly mid-point on the back, while the second is found just above the teeth. In section the comb tapers gradually from the upper edge of the back to the finely cut teeth. To produce this taper involved much work, as revealed by the comb blank, **I-69**, discussed below with other 'workshop material' (p. 40). Standard undecorated combs varied somewhat in size and shape. This is certainly true of examples found on the acropolis (Poursat 1977*b*, pl. III) and in the Citadel House Area. Comb **I-4** — which lacks only a thin sliver from one vertical edge — is rather small and almost square in shape (Fig. 2). Although **I-5** and **I-6** are broken along one vertical edge, it is clear that originally they were much more rectangular (Figs. 7, 8). **I-6** is somewhat unusual in being pierced near its upper edge (cf. Poursat 1977*b*, cat. no. 38). The tiny fragment **I-7** (Fig. 8) offers an interesting variation on the standard type, since here the teeth are thicker than the 'back'. Presumably this element would have been inserted into a separate handle. A more complete example from Tiryns (IvTir cat. no. 7) provides confirmation, as it is scored along the narrow 'back'. In fact, given the danger of damaging ivory teeth, it is a trifle surprising this solution was not adopted more often. An ivory comb back, with slot to receive teeth, comes from the chamber tombs (Poursat 1977*b*, cat. no. 266, pl. XXIII). Perhaps, in this case, the teeth were wood.

Spoons were rarely made of ivory and related materials during the Aegean Bronze Age and no uniform type exists (see p. 141). Our example (**I-8**, Fig. 5, Pl. 5) therefore provides a welcome addition to the repertoire. The original purpose may have been cosmetic rather than culinary, given the material and high quality of finish. However, it may have sustained its damage before the phase VII catastrophe; if so, its presence alongside salvaged items and workshop material in Room 32 would make sense (see Fig. 5). Alternatively, we might interpret the spoon as an offering in the Room with the Fresco Complex (cf. **I-9**).

This explanation certainly seems appropriate for the finely worked cosmetic implement (**I-9**), found in the bowl (68-1402) containing numerous beads and trinkets in Room 19 (above p. 7; *WBM* 10, 18–19, fig. 5). Carved in the shape of a human arm with clenched fist, one end terminates in a small flat bowl (Fig. 2, Pl. 5). Two unpublished examples exist on Crete, found in LM III tombs at Milatos and Phylaki Apokoronou (p. 142). Similar in concept is an item from T. XXIV at Argos, while a gold 'ear-pick' was recovered in ChT 55 at Mycenae (see p. 142). Exactly how these items were used remains open to question. Although **I-9** offers no further insights, it makes a welcome addition to the corpus.

Several more objects in this category also come from Room 19. A pair of enigmatic pieces, tentatively identified as a small box-lid and fastener (**I-10**, Fig. 2), was found on the other side of the room from the bowl with the offerings (*WBM* 10, 23–4, fig. 7). Associated with the 'lid' were two small beads (68-1605) of carnelian and faience. Unfortunately, no parallels exist which might help elucidate the original shape of the object, much less its place of manufacture. A small double globular bead (**I?-11,** Fig. 2) decorated with incision, found in bowl 68-1402, was originally classed as ivory. However, this identification is by no means certain and a vitreous material (frit, faience or glass) seems more likely (cf. 68-1524: *WBM* 10, 19, fig. 5). Indeed, ivory and bone were not favoured for items of personal adornment (beads, amulets or seals) after the pre-palatial period on Crete. Of course we cannot be certain that **I?-11** was made in the Aegean. It does not conform to any common Mycenaean bead type and the presence of other exotica in the Room 19 deposit (*WBM* 10, 18–19) should alert us to the possibility that **I?-11** is an import. As for **I-12** (Fig. 2), a fragmentary conulus or button, little can be said. It too is unparalleled — at least in ivory, although two steatite conuli were found in Room 19 and many more were recovered in the Room with the Fresco Complex.

With several ivories found in phase VIII contexts, we return to more familiar Mycenaean types. The first (**I-13**, Pl. 5) is a finely worked figure-of-eight shield, which probably served as a pendant or toggle. Flat in section and undecorated, the underside has a narrow strip or strap, which is pierced laterally. Poursat discussed shields of this type, which he termed *à poignée*, but failed to draw a distinction between them and the more familiar shields used as appliqués on furniture (Poursat 1977*a*, 98–100). The latter are usually decorated in low relief, are markedly convex in section, and have mortises for attachment on the underside. They are frequently recovered in groups and are sometimes associated with massed compositions, such as footstools (Poursat 1977*a*, 31–3, pl. VII.3). The shields *à poignée* are entirely different. The distinctive strip on the underside supports the view that the item was threaded onto a thong or leather strap (*BSA* 68, 339–40; *BSA* 52, 209). Unlike the relief appliqués, shields *à poignée* tend to be found singly. The type has a long history, originating on Crete. A small example made of lapis lazuli was found by Evans at Knossos and dated to MM II (Evans 1930, 315, fig. 207). An ivory shield from the Royal Road, Knossos (*AR* 1957, 22) certainly belongs to this type. Further comparanda, including new examples from Tiryns and Midea, are listed on p. 147.

PLATE 5

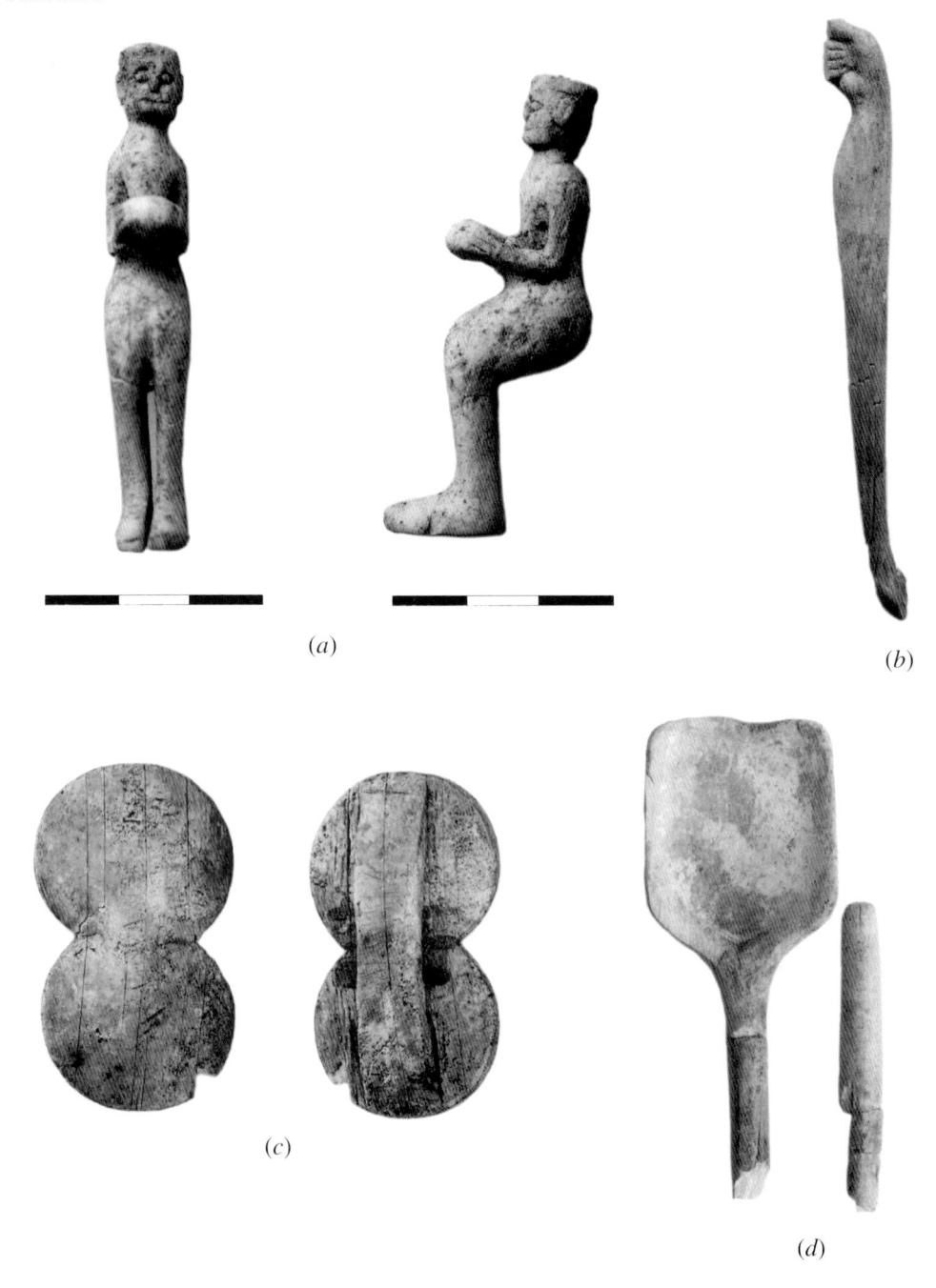

(a)

(b)

(c)

(d)

(*a*) Figurine **I-3**. Cosmetic articles: (*b*) cosmetic implement **I-9**; (*c*) pendant or toggle in shape of figure-of-eight shield **I-13**; (*d*) spoon **I-8**. Scale: 1:1.

The last three items in this category survive as fragments only (Fig. 7). **I-14** undoubtedly represents part of a toggle, similar in shape to modern examples. Though not particularly common, the type is attested in both ivory and metal during LM/LH II–III (see p. 148). **I-15**, broken at both ends, is part of a pin or needle; **I-16** is a needle fragment. These are noteworthy only because both are made from ivory. Although many Mycenaean pins and needles are so described, in reality most are made from bone (below p. 62 f).

Other functional items

Most objects in this category can be readily understood as components of objects made in other materials, e.g. pommels and other accoutrements for swords, daggers, or knives. The enhancing of weaponry with imported ivory goes back to pre-palatial Crete and on the mainland was one of the earliest uses of ivory in the Shaft Grave era (Krzyszkowska 1988, 228–9, 230–1; Poursat 1977*a*, 35–6). However, in the Late Mycenaean period ivory pommels are not common and so the examples from the Citadel House Area (**I-17** and **I-18**) are welcome. In addition there is a small pommel or knob (**I-19**), a pair of Naue II hilt-plates (**I-20** and **I-21**) and a possible knife handle (**I-22**). In this category are also included several other 'functional' items (**I-23** to **I-25**), though what purpose they served is more problematic.

Most pommels, whether made of ivory or stone, are shaped like mushrooms, having a domed 'cap' and a short neck. While pommel **I-17** conforms to these expectations, **I-18** is rather ovoid in plan and flat in section (Pl. 6). Since it has sustained damage and is now made up in wax, one cannot be sure how far (if at all) it originally departed from the norm. It was found in the phase VIII destruction debris associated with the Causeway Deposit, close to the entrance of Room 6 (above p. 14). Several stone pommels also come from similarly uninformative contexts — phase VIII debris in open areas or passages (*WBM* 27, 23, fig. 11, pl. 3, cat. nos. 39, 40, 42). By contrast, the large and fine pommel **I-17** (Fig. 3, Pl. 6) was found on the altar in Room 31, along with the lion (**I-2**) and Minoan stone bowl (above pp. 21, 24; *WBM* 27, 6, fig. 1, cat. no. 3). It is reasonable to regard it as a votive. Whether this should be construed as a case of offering *pars pro toto* is not certain. An intriguing parallel for the deposition of detached sword pommels does occur at Midea. Modifications to the megaron in early LH IIIC created a niche, in which were found faience beads, a glass plaque and three intact pommels: of ivory, alabaster and lapis lacedaimonius (*OpAth* 21, 1996, 30–1, fig. 66). While the Midea pommels are surely older than their context, we cannot judge how much older. Likewise there is no way of dating **I-17** from Room 31. In any case, its sword may have been damaged and the bronze needed for re-cycling. Thus we cannot be sure that there was a special symbolic link between the pommel and the iconography of the fresco, with its sword-bearing female figure (*WBM* 29, in preparation).

The original function of **I-19** (Fig. 5), a small onion-shaped knob, is not clear. In common with pommels it has a square-cut mortise on the underside, but lacks any rivet-holes for securing it to the tang of a weapon. The slightly pointed apex would make a less comfortable grip than the normal dome-shape of pommels. However, in the absence of parallels certainty is impossible. The small size is not diagnostic. As alternative interpretations one might suggest a knob for a chest or even a finial for a piece of furniture. Since there is old damage in and around the mortise on the underside, the item was evidently salvaged. The same is also true of the Naue II hilt-plates (**I-20** and **I-21**, Fig. 5, Pl. 6) whose identity and chronological significance were first recognized by Diana Wardle.[2] The rivet-holes are stained from bronze and two rivets survive

PLATE 6

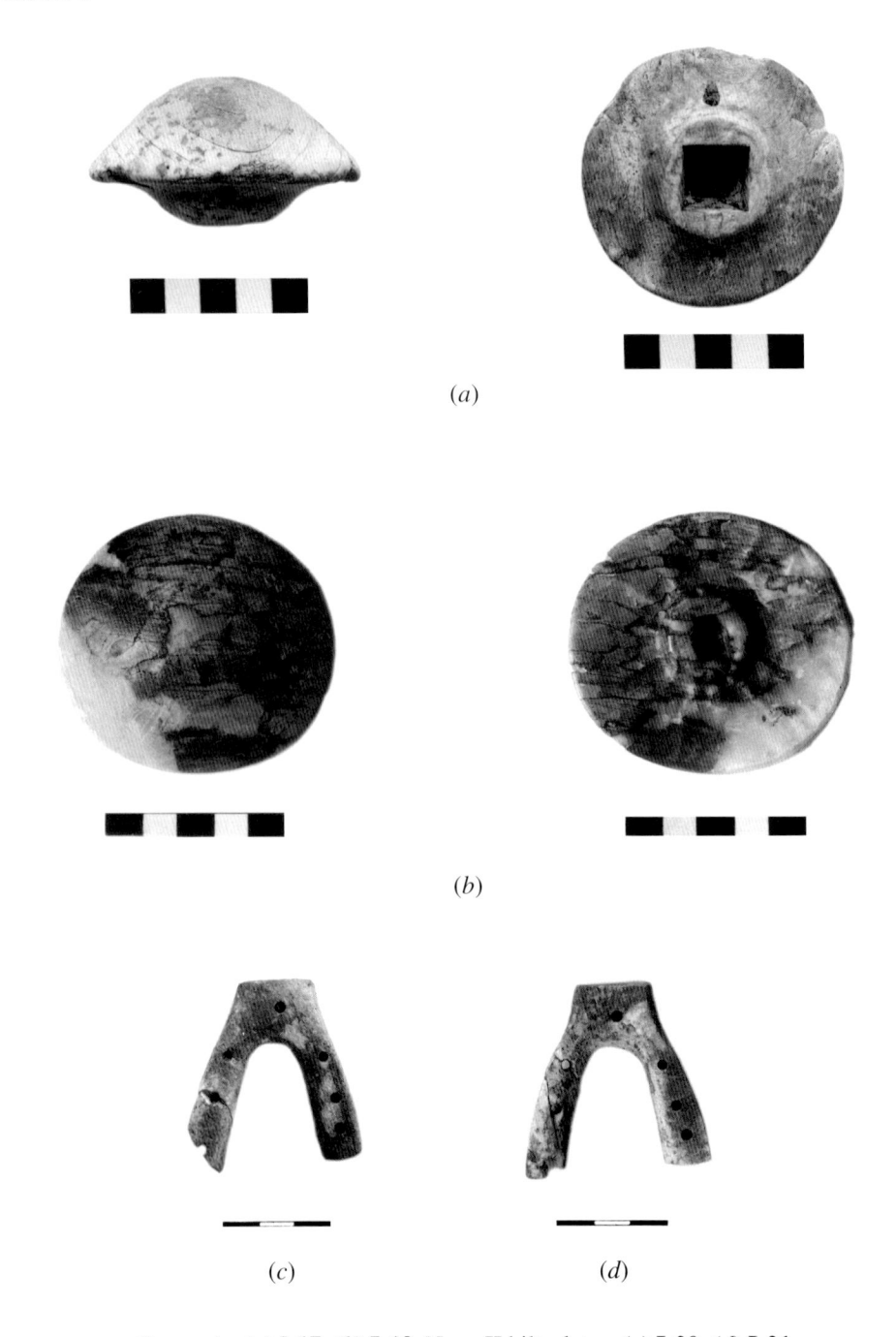

(a)

(b)

(c) (d)

Pommels: (a) **I-17**; (b) **I-18**. Naue II hilt-plates: (c) **I-20**; (d) **I-21**.

(loose). In addition, **I-20** also shows signs of (an earlier?) repair, as there are two small drillings in the broken edge of one prong (Fig. 5). Ivory hilt-plates for a Naue II sword are (to my knowledge) otherwise unparalleled, although this may be an accident of preservation. For this reason alone they are important. Moreover, the secure phase VII (mid LH IIIB) date proves that this sword type was indeed current in the Mycenaean world well before the end of the 13th century BC. A complete Naue II sword was found by Schliemann on the acropolis in the House of the Warrior Vase, but lacks a secure context (see p. 157 for references). Our salvaged hilt-plates (as well as knob **I-19**) were found with other kinds of ivory 'workshop material' in Room 32, the small storeroom-cum-shrine adjacent to the Room with the Fresco (p. 9; see also below pp. 36, 38). A similar range of material was recovered in basement Room II, including **I-22**, which is apparently a knife handle, broken at the first rivet (Fig. 4). Whether this was damaged during manufacture or at a later stage cannot be determined. In any case, it too may have been retained as salvage. An intact handle (**B/I-1**, Fig. 12), still attached to its blade, was found in Room 7 (phase VIII). Although knife handles made of bone or ivory are attested in the Mycenaean period, those that remain attached to their blades are usually in poor condition. In such cases, distinguishing bone from ivory can prove difficult.

Three more items in this category belong to well-known — but enigmatic — types. The first (**I-23**, Fig. 3) is a so-called *pièce de lyre*, which has parallels elsewhere at Mycenae, as well as Menidi, Spata and now Tiryns (see p. 163). The tholos at Menidi also yielded parts of upright 'arms' and transverse bars with holes for attaching the strings (Poursat 1977*b*, cat. nos. 425, 426, pl. XLV). They seem to belong to two separate instruments, although the reconstruction in the National Museum, Athens, is open to question. Especially problematic is the function of the *pièces de lyre*. Although these are thought to have secured and tightened the strings, it is not easy to see how this was effected. The poor condition of the Menidi lyre(s) and the fact that *pièces de lyre* are usually recovered singly further impedes investigation. Unfortunately **I-23**, a rather small and undistinguished example, offers no insights. Although found in Room 31, it should probably be associated with the salvaged items and other workshop material from Room 32.

Another perplexing object is **I-24**, shaped rather like an elongated acorn, with an offset cap (Fig. 7). Singletons are known from the ChTs (1887/88) and the acropolis; another was recently recovered at Tiryns (see p. 165). Only at Thebes do they occur in a group, but the examples found in the 'Treasure Room' give no direct clues as to their use (but see **I-25** below). Poursat has pointed to Egyptian parallels, thought to have been 'stoppers' (Poursat 1977*a*, 38–9; G. Brunton, *Matmar* (London 1948), 19). If form is indeed a reliable guide to function, then this explanation is plausible. But questions remain. Why are there so few? Why has none been found in the mouth of a vessel? Were pierced examples (including **I-24**) tied on to ensure they were not lost when removed for pouring? Sadly, our piece (from phase VIII destruction debris over Room 7) provides no answers.

The fragment **I-25** (Fig. 8) belongs to another familiar Mycenaean type, for which no satisfactory explanation exists. Conventionally known as 'candlesticks', they continue to perplex 40 years after Wace's original discussion (*Archaeology* 1960, 40–3; Poursat 1977*a*, 40–1; Tournavitou 1995, 180–1, pl. 25). The idea that they served some kind of religious purpose, e.g. as offering tables, cannot be ruled out, but no corroboration exists. And less elaborate examples in terracotta and bronze provide few additional insights. A new ivory example from Thebes has prompted Aravantinos to re-interpret 'candlesticks' and 'acorn-shaped' objects as horse-trappings (Aravantinos 2000, 60–70, figs. 23–5, 36–7). Unfortunately **I-25**, found with disturbed LH IIIC material, adds nothing to the debate.

Two more items **I-53** and **I-54** may once have been components of functional objects. However, their condition is now so poor that their original shapes cannot be ascertained, much less their purpose. They are included below (p. 36) with other indeterminate objects.

Furniture decorations: appliqués and inlays

The most important use of ivory in the LBA Aegean was to decorate wooden furniture and chests (Krzyszkowska 1996, 99–102). By LH IIIA–B the repertoire had come to include three main kinds of product. The finest pieces are the plaques carved in low relief, usually with representational scenes. Appliqués are generally individual motifs — figure-of-eight shields, warrior heads, columns — carved in relief and designed to stand proud of the surface they decorated. They were held in place with dowels and mortises, assisted by adhesives. During LH IIIA–B most inlays were cut-out shapes (e.g. lilies, rosettes, ivy) decorated with incision. Plain strips of varying widths and ribbed borders are also well attested. Adhesives, simple pegs or occasionally small mortises served to fix the pieces in place. Appliqués and inlays are often recovered in groups and were clearly used in mass compositions, e.g. on 'footstools'. Especially large numbers were recovered in the Kadmeion at Thebes (Symeonoglou 1973, 53, 59–61) and also in the Houses outside the Citadel at Mycenae (Tournavitou 1995). In both cases we are apparently dealing with storerooms for workshops involved in the manufacture, assembly and perhaps restoration of fine furniture.

Set against this backdrop the finds from the Citadel House Area are, at first sight, disappointing. No relief plaques or conventional appliqués were found and the inlays are humdrum lilies, rosettes and strips. But on closer scrutiny the collection proves to contain a number of intriguing items. This is certainly true of our first piece (**I-26,** Fig. 7, Pl. 7*a*) an unusually large appliqué, which *seems* to represent a dagger. Since it is incomplete, badly burnt and restored in wax, it is difficult to identify the motif with confidence. In ivory there are no parallels, however remote, to help us understand it. Among actual weapons, the short dirk (Type H) — with its horned hilts and rather broad ribbed blade — seems to offer the best comparison (Sandars, *AJA* 67, 1963, pl. 27: 52–3). It may, of course, be wrong to seek an exact match — most motifs employed by Mycenaean craftsmen are stylized to a greater or lesser extent. At least the function of the piece is clear: like other appliqués its upper surface is decorated in relief, while the underside is scored and provided with mortises for attachment to a wooden backing. The 'dagger' was found in the phase VIII destruction debris in Room 7. The floor deposit in this room also yielded two more ivories, both of uncertain type: a possible appliqué (**I-52**) and a roughly rectangular slab or plaque (**I-53**). These are included with other indeterminate pieces, below.

The ribbed appliqué (**I-27**, Fig. 7) with chamfered end probably served as a border piece. As preserved it has two mortises (one rectangular, another round) on the underside, but is not scored. It comes from collapse and wash levels over Room 18.

Two more items in this category are certainly components of wooden furniture, though exactly how they were used remains unclear. The first (**I-28**) seems to be designed as a corner piece, since at least two faces look finished (Fig. 3, Pl. 7*b–d*). The principal face has finely carved fluting, while the second is smooth and concave. Deep circular mortises and heavy scoring on the underside served for attachment. It is, however, far from certain that this piece

PLATE 7

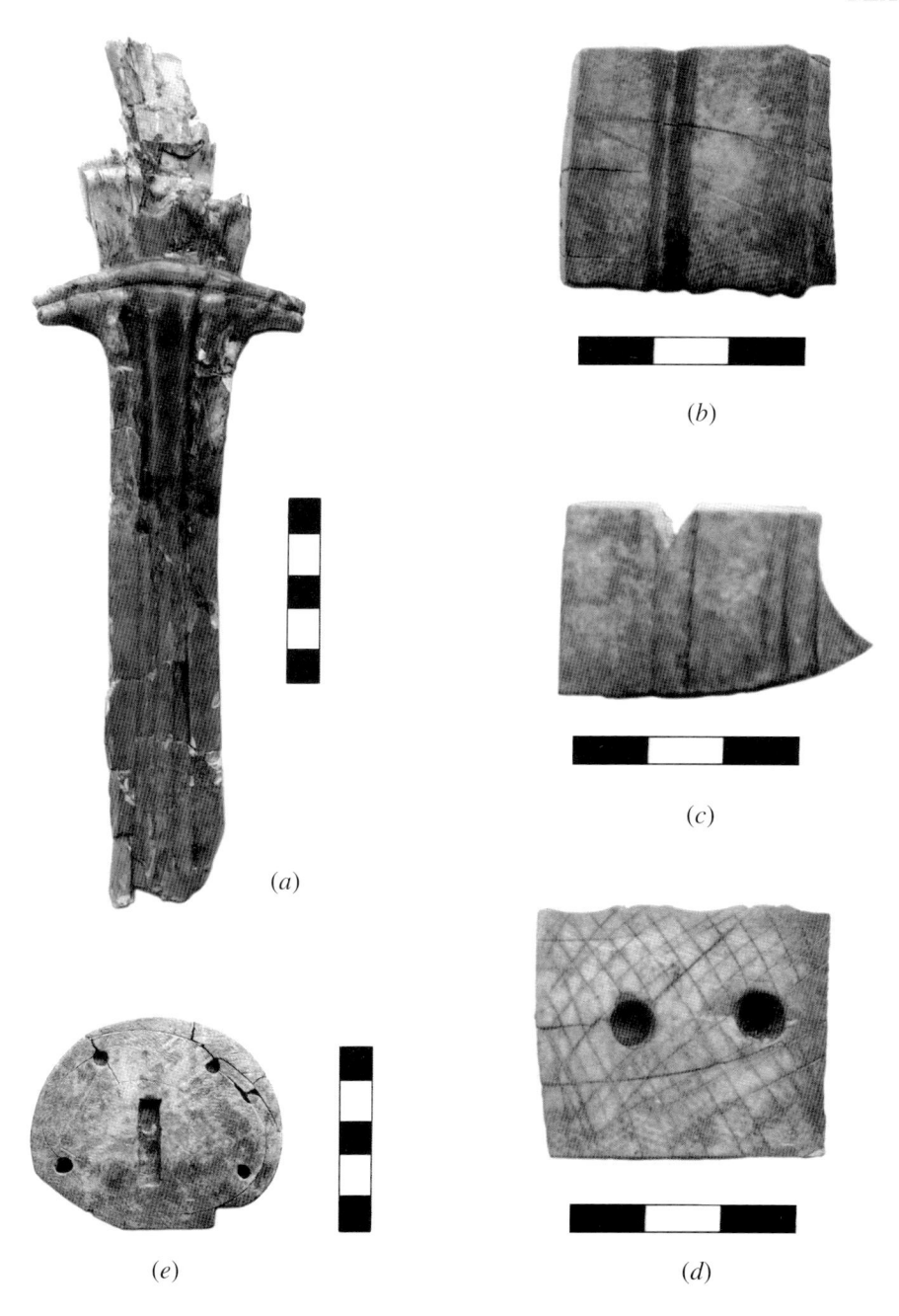

Appliqués: (*a*) 'dagger' **I-26** (upper surface); moulding **I-28**: (*b*) Face A, (*c*) Face B, (*d*) Face C; (*e*) oval attachment **I-29**.

was in use at the time of the phase VII catastophe. Although found in Room 31, it may well be a stray from the 'workshop material' stored in Room 32. The same perhaps also applies to **I-29** (Fig. 8, Pl. 7*e*) an oval appliqué, associated with early LH IIIC material in the upper fill of Room 33. This, too, is an interesting piece for which parallels exist at Pylos and Tiryns (see p. 175). Each is undecorated, but possesses an especially complex system of mortises. Their placement suggests that the pieces were to be attached or inset vertically (Krzyszkowska 1996, 101, fig. 6.2).

Although **I-28** and **I-29** were not necessarily in use at the time of the phase VII catastrophe, they do appear to be finished objects. By contrast several more items — probably intended as appliqués or furniture components — appear to be unfinished. They include **I-60** found in Room II and **I-63** and **I-64** from Area 36 and perhaps also **I-61** and **I-62** from Room 32. These will be considered below.

The remaining items in this category are inlays (Pl. 8). Our first group comprises plain strips of varying widths: narrow, **I-30** to **I-36** (W. 0.006–0.01 m); medium, **I-37** to **I-40** (W. *c.* 0.015–0.02 m); and wide, **I-41** (W. 0.028 m). Most are broken at both ends, but several are complete: **I-33**, **I-34** and **I-41**. These measure about 10 cm long. A long strip of medium width (**I-38**, Fig. 6) from Area 36 is twice as long and is also rather thick. One long edge is scored, suggesting that the piece abutted a wooden frame. Moreover, two rectangular mortises are cut in from this edge to assist attachment. One of the narrow inlays (**I-31**, Fig. 4) from Room II is also noteworthy for its exceptional length (over 25 cm). This example has a rather uneven section and traces of tool marks on the upper surface. Similar tell-tale signs occur in other examples, e.g. guidelines remaining along the edges, rough corners and the like. We might expect such minor imperfections to be rectified during assembly, when final adjustments and polishing would be done. Of course had the strips been found in residential quarters, we would be forced to conclude they were in use at the time of the catastrophe. However, the examples from Rooms II, 32 and Area 36 were associated with 'workshop material' (Figs. 4–6; and below p. 38). Perhaps they were being stored pending assembly or were left over from larger job-lots. The same also seems true of the lily and rosette inlays found in Room II (see below). One or two narrow strips (e.g. **I-35** and **I-36**, Fig. 8) do appear to be finished, though as singletons from earlier (phase VI) and later (phase X) contexts they are uninformative.

While plain inlay strips are well attested on Crete from the proto-palatial period onwards, cut-out inlays with incised decoration only came into their own during LH IIIA–B. Rosettes and lilies are especially common: hundreds were found in the 'Ivory Houses' outside the Citadel (Tournavitou 1995, 143; 145). Our collection is very much smaller, comprising about two dozen rosettes (**I-42** to **I-44**) and lilies (**I-45** to **I-48**) *in toto*. Almost all came from Room II (see Fig. 4 for a selection). While the rosettes are unremarkable, the lilies are rather interesting, since no two examples match. Some volutes are executed with precision, others are sloppy; in every case the incised lines were executed in a different order. In a mass composition, these minor discrepancies might have passed unnoticed. But as with the inlay strips, there is reason to question whether these cut-out inlays were actually in use (decorating a box) at the time of the catastrophe. Items of this kind were surely ordered and produced in large job-lots. Indeed, this is supported by the large numbers found in the 'Ivory Houses', where even greater variations are encountered among the rosettes and lilies (Tournavitou 1995,143–8, figs. 27, 28). In cases of serial production, left-overs and rejects would certainly be expected. That mistakes occurred is demonstrated by **I-46h**, which had been turned over and re-worked — more successfully — on

PLATE 8

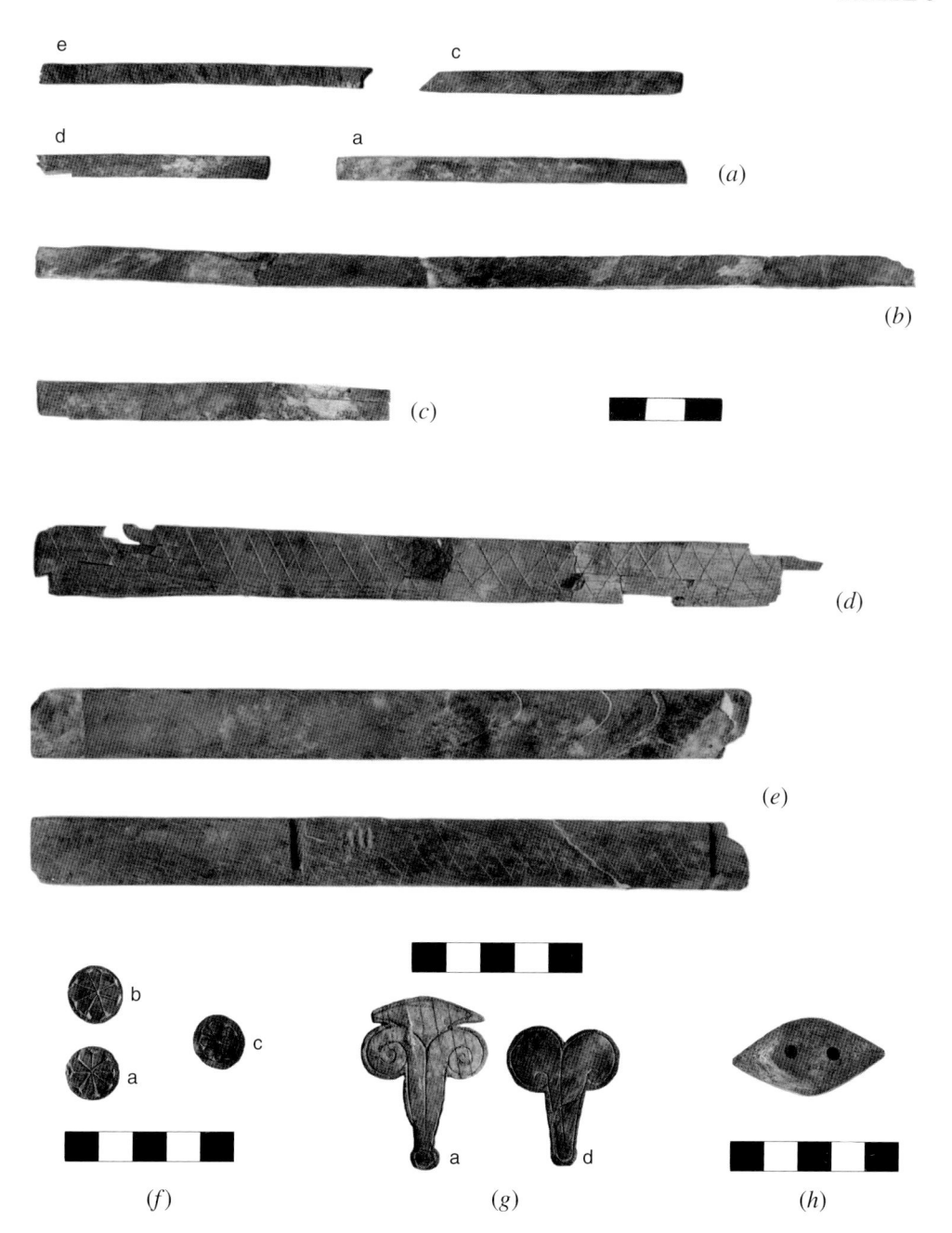

Inlays: (*a*) **I-30**; (*b*) **I-31**; (*c*) **I-34**; (*d*) **I-37**, underside; (*e*) **I-38**, upper surface (*above*), underside (*below*); (*f*) **I-43**; (*g*) **I-46**; (*h*) **I-49**. Scale 1:2.

35

the other side (Fig. 4; cf. Tournavitou 1995, pl. 18c, d). Finally, it is worth noting that in our collection, only two lilies have a waz, all the rest belong to the simple variety.

Of our remaining inlays there is little to be said. One (**I-49**, Fig. 4), in the shape of a diamond, has mortises on the underside rather like an appliqué, but its bevelled edges indicate it was meant to be inset. Found in Room II, it has no close parallels. Likewise, the T-shaped inlay (?), **I-50**, is hard to match in other collections. This was found on the LH IIIC early floor of Room xxxiv (over Area 36) and is likely to be a stray from phase VII (Fig. 8). In addition a fragmentary incised disc (**I-51**) was recovered with LH IIIC material from Enclosure cd/cc (Fig. 8).

Indeterminate objects and fragments

Every site has its share of objects that defy identification due to excessive damage and lack of comparanda. Our uncertain pieces fall into two groups. The first were obviously sizeable objects in use at the time of the phase VIII destruction, but which are now so badly burnt and distorted that their original shapes cannot be retrieved. The first (**I-52**, Fig. 7) was evidently an appliqué, since there are circular and sloping mortises on the underside. The second (**I-53**, Pl. 9*a*) is a large slab, nearly rectangular, with an offset ledge, perhaps belonging to a piece of furniture or a box. Both come from South House Annex Room 7. The third piece (**I-54**, Pl. 9*b*–*c*) is truly puzzling. This curving segment with thick moulded edge was originally identified as part of a rhyton or pyxis (*BSA* 68, 340). Perhaps, although parallels are lacking. Moreover it is uncertain whether the lateral edges are clean breaks or worked surfaces. If the latter, then **I-54** may have been a component or decoration of some kind. Since the lower edge is certainly worked, it cannot be a broken *peigne à coiffure* as Poursat thought (1977*a*, 39). The remaining items are very much smaller and, if anything, more indeterminate. One or two (**I-55**, **I-56?**) might be parts of inlays: along with a small fragment **I-57**, they were found in Room II (phase VII). An amorphous fragment (**I-58**) comes from early LH IIIC levelling in Room xxiv, while three small bits (**I-59**) were recovered in year-surface cleaning.

Partly worked ivory

Almost one-third of the ivories found in the Citadel House Area fall into this category. The collection is significant on several counts. Substantial in quantity and varied in character, the material offers important insights into Mycenaean ivory working. Moreover, unlike other examples of partly worked ivory from Mycenae (see below pp. 50–1), our pieces come from securely dated find-spots. Most were recovered from phase VII deposits, though there are a few later strays. Nevertheless, the presence of this material on the site is hard to explain and individual pieces can be difficult to interpret (Krzyszkowska 1992*a*; 1997).

Even terminology represents challenge. The expression 'partly worked ivory' may be cumbersome, but is less ambiguous than other terms in use (Krzyszkowska 1992*a*, esp. n. 1). 'Raw ivory', if used at all, is best reserved for unworked tusks. 'Worked ivory' is confusing, since it is sometimes applied to finished objects (e.g. 'a group of ivories, worked and partly worked', *WBM* 1, 49). Still more unsatisfactory as a generic term is 'unfinished', for this implies that the item could achieve a final usable state with additional work. It may be appropriate for blanks or rough-outs, where the form of the finished object is beginning to emerge. But 'unfinished' simply will not do for irregular off-cuts, which result from primary or secondary sectioning of the tusk, much less for small pieces of scrap and *débitage* (chips). In other cases, items may be unfinished because mistakes were made during the course of manufacture and

PLATE 9

(a)

(b)

(c)

Indeterminate objects: (*a*) rectangular slab **I-53**; (*b*–*c*) segment with moulding **I-54**.

further work was abandoned. And finally, there are items that may be all but finished, which would have been finally trimmed or polished at the time of assembly. If, for one reason or another, they were never assembled — how should we designate them? The numerous strips and cut-out inlays from Room II are prime examples (see above pp. 6, 34–6). With some misgivings I catalogued them as finished objects — usable at a pinch, though probably never used. Then there are other pieces which certainly *had been* used, but were obviously not in use at the time of deposition. The Naue II hilt-plates (**I-20**, **I-21**) and small knob (**I-19**) from Room 32 meet these criteria, and there are other more equivocal pieces of salvage (**I-8**, **I-22**, **I-23**). Needless to say, there are also items which defy any adequate interpretation. When it is neither practical nor desirable to be precise, the term 'workshop material' can be a useful collective (Krzyszkowska 1997).

To evaluate partly worked ivory is obviously no easy task (Krzyszkowska 1992*a*). Essential is a sound understanding of ivory in its unworked state. The shape and size of tusks, natural features such as the outer surface or 'bark' and pulp cavity, the properties of the ivory itself — all these need to be taken into account. Potential end-products must also be kept in mind, for these might well determine how the tusk was initially sectioned. Secondary sectioning to produce rough-outs and blanks will certainly yield off-cuts of various shapes and sizes. Later stages in working — when finished objects begin to take their final form — will also produce various kinds of waste. Tiny irregular chips suggest carving (in the round or in relief), while more regular trimmings point to inlay manufacture. It is worth re-iterating here that no single site has ever yielded a complete range of workshop material from unworked tusks to finished products by way of rough-outs and blanks and with a full complement of waste and *débitage* (Krzyszkowska 1992*a*; 1997). Thus any attempt to identify specific processes or to reconstruct workshop practices more generally is bound to be somewhat speculative. Among our pieces, however, it is possible to isolate several groups: unfinished items (**I-60** to **I-65**), blanks (**I-66** to **I-69**), pieces from primary and secondary sectioning (**I-70** to **I-75**), irregular off-cuts and waste (**I-76** to **I-83**). But it must be stressed that the groupings should be regarded as tentative.

The unfinished items (**I-60** to **I-65**) are especially difficult to assess, since they do not match known types. We face further obstacles when pieces are broken, as is the case with **I-60**, found in Room II. Originally the object may have been T-shaped in plan, although the lower part of the 'stem' is missing (Fig. 4, Pl. 10). The upper bar of the T is decorated with shallow ribbing and has three mortises cut through to the underside. On the upper surface of the 'stem' two arc shaped areas have been produced by cutting down the ivory. Were insets in another material intended? Also puzzling is the upper edge of the bar. At one end (A) it is neatly cut with a square edge and a rectangular section, yet here the ribbing is irregular. There is a marked taper toward the other end (B), where the section is irregular, but the ribbing neater. Moreover, toward end B and in the central part of the 'stem' the underside has been roughly bevelled, i.e. attempts have been made to reduce the thickness of the object. But are these features enough to warrant the term 'unfinished'? Were the object complete might we not reach a different conclusion? Perhaps. The small inlays found in Room II have already underscored the difficulties we face in deciding acceptable standards of finish. **I-60** seems to display a series of slight miscalculations, which may have needed adjustment for the piece to fit a particular composition or article of furniture. In my view, the modifications were probably not complete and the piece was not used. It is also possible that re-working was a failure and **I-60** was retained for its scrap value.

PLATE 10

Partly worked ivories. Unfinished objects: (*a*) **I-60**, upper surface; (*b*) **I-61**; (*c*–*d*) **I-62**; (*e*) **I-65**; (*f*) **I-64**, upper surface.

This interpretation may also apply to two unfinished pieces found in Room 32. **I-61** is a very flat quadrangular plaque with tool marks on both faces (Fig. 5, Pl. 10*b*). Although three edges are cut evenly to form near right-angles, the fourth edge is irregular. Here the ivory has split naturally along the lamellae. In an attempt to rectify the damage, 15 triangular notches were cut into the edge, apparently to facilitate a join. There is no sign of a matching piece, so presumably the repair work had not been started. Indeed one wonders whether *any* repair to **I-61** would have been satisfactory. A much better option would have been to trim off the split edge to provide blanks for inlay manufacture. Harder to understand is the large wedge-shaped piece of ivory **I-62**, which has one curving moulded edge (Fig. 5, Pl. 10*c–d*). Circular mortises indicate that **I-62** was to be joined to at least two more pieces, presumably with similar moulding. Was this the original intention or another attempt to rectify an error? The eventual end-product remains a complete mystery. Certainly not a pyxis lid or base: when these are made in two parts, the join is always straight (i.e. across the diameter). Moreover, the blanks for lids and bases are invariably cut lengthwise from the tusk; **I-62** is cut transversely. Whatever the aim, it seems that work on the object was abandoned; perhaps the damaged moulding was a factor.

Two more unfinished pieces were found above the phase VII floor in Area 36 (Fig. 6). **I-63** is a small plaque, apparently damaged during manufacture and, perhaps, abandoned. The same explanation may also apply to **I-64** (Pl. 10*f*), a curious object shaped rather like a mushroom. Since it has no parallels, it is difficult to guess the likely end-product. Perhaps it was meant to be an appliqué or furniture decoration, though there are no mortises on the underside. Our last piece in this group (**I-65**, Fig. 8, Pl. 10*e*) is also difficult to explain. At first sight it looks like a small wedge-shaped off-cut, but two surfaces are carefully worked and reasonably well finished. That said, it seems unlikely that the piece could be used in its present form. Although found with phase IX material above Room 31, it is surely a stray from the main phase VII deposit in Room 32.

Happily, our next five objects (**I-66** to **I-69**) are much easier to comprehend. Two items found in Room II are undoubtedly blanks for wide inlay strips (**I-66a–b**, Fig. 4, Pl. 11*a*). Although they have been given mitred ends, the long edges still need some trimming (traces of a guide remain on **I-66b**). Heavy tool marks remain on both and these would obviously need to be smoothed and polished before the pieces could be used. **I-67** from Room II, along with its close match **I-68** from Room 32, is quadrangular in plan, tapering slightly toward one end (Figs. 4, 5, Pl. 11*b–c*). Since they seem to have been shaped quite deliberately, it is reasonable to regard them as blanks. Among finished ivories, knife handles provide the most plausible parallels (cf. **I-22**, Fig. 4). The last of our blanks was certainly intended for a comb (**I-69**, Fig. 7, Pl. 12*a–b*). Here the carver has started with a flat blank, cut lengthwise from the tusk, standard procedure for many Mycenaean ivories (Krzyszkowska 1992*a*). Indeed relief plaques, inlays, pyxis lids and combs all begin as flat rectangular blanks. But here a rough horizontal guideline has been cut across Face A and the surface worked down with a serrated implement to achieve a tapering section. Face B, less well preserved, shows similar tool marks. Once the surface had been suitably prepared, the teeth would have been cut. **I-69** is our only example of partly worked ivory from phase VIII and was found near the entrance to Room 1. It is very unfortunate, indeed, that such an important piece does not come from a more informative context.

Probably the most remarkable piece of partly worked ivory from the site is the large cube (**I-70**) found in Room 32 (Pl. 13). This certainly reflects an early stage in manufacture, not far removed from primary sectioning of the tusk.[3] The base of the block (**B**) represents a transverse

PLATE 11

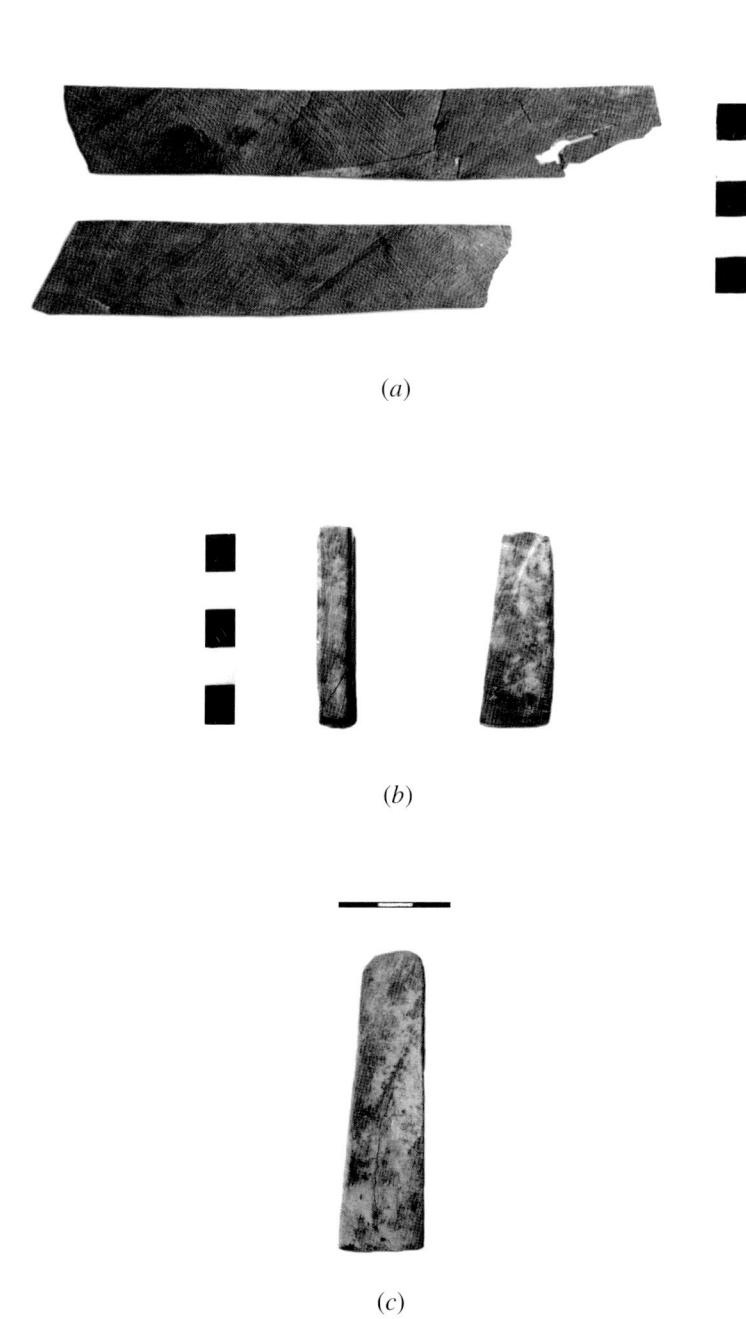

(*a*)

(*b*)

(*c*)

Partly worked ivories. Blanks: (*a*) **I-66**; (*b*) **I-67**; (*c*) **I-68**.

PLATE 12

(*a*)

(*b*)

Ivory comb blank **I-69**: (*a*) Face A; (*b*) Face B. Scale 3:4.

PLATE 13

(*a*)

(*b*)

(*c*)

(*d*)

(*e*)

Partly worked ivory cube **I-70**: (*a*) 'main' Face E; (*b*) 'inner' Face D; (*c*) Base B; (*d*) 'outer' Face (natural surface) C; (*e*) Face F. (See p. 257 for decayed 'top' Face A.) Arrows mark pulp cavity. Fig. 9 (*a*) shows how **I-70** was cut from the tusk.

section from the natural outer surface (**C**) to the pulp cavity in the centre (Fig. 9*a*). Traces of this feature help to explain why the tusk was sectioned at this particular point. By using a flexible rod or reed, the carver would be able to gauge where the pulp cavity ended, and hence where to make his initial cut. Obviously there was much usable ivory in the proximal end, which contains the tapering pulp cavity. But only from regular blocks like **I-70** could flat rectangular blanks be readily cut. These would be removed rather like slices of bread from a loaf, eventually leaving behind a 'crust' in the form of the natural outer surface (cf. **I-77**; Krzyszkowska 1992*a*, 26). It is possible that some blanks had already been removed from **I-70**, but it would certainly yield more. Indeed, it is the closest thing to 'primary' raw material on the site. Other pieces seem to be waste from secondary sectioning and are often too small or irregularly shaped to be of much further value. A good parallel for our block exists among the ivories found by Schliemann on the acropolis. Although about half the size of **I-70**, the shape is comparable and it also preserves the natural outer surface (Krzyszkowska 1992*a*, 26, pl. 1d).

Primary sectioning will also entail the removal of the tusk tip, which is marred by fine cracks and has an awkward shape. For this reason the tips are usually waste pieces, although they might supply small pieces of ivory for secondary manufacture, e.g. dowels, pegs and the like. One wonders whether our example **I-71** was destined for further working, since near the base the tip had been squared off (Fig. 8, Pl. 14*a*). Coming as it does from the levelling in early LH IIIC in Room 33, **I-71** surely belongs with the main phase VII deposit in Room 32 or Area 36. Other examples of tusk tips are known from Knossos, Tiryns and the Shaft Graves at Mycenae (see p. 258).

Three more pieces may be associated with secondary sectioning of the tusk, in particular removing natural features to obtain blanks of suitable shape (Fig. 5). **I-72** is a large wedge-shaped segment, preserving the natural outer surface on one face (Pl. 14*b*). This feature also occurs on a long and narrow wedge **I-74** (Pl. 14*f–h*). Part of the pulp cavity runs along the edge of the large wedge **I-73** (Fig. 9b, Pl. 14*c–e*). One wonders whether these segments could have been used for secondary manufacture. By the time they were trimmed down to a regular shape and section, not much usable ivory would remain. The same is certainly true for **I-75** (Fig. 5, Pl. 15*a*) an irregular off-cut. All these pieces were found in Room 32. Although no exact parallels exist (indeed that would be surprising) similar kinds of off-cuts have been found elsewhere, notably on the acropolis at Mycenae and at Tiryns (see pp. 261, 263 for further references and general discussion in Krzyszkowska 1992*a*).

Our remaining segments seem to be waste pure and simple. At first sight **I-76**, found in Room 32, looks as though it might be a blank for a rectangular plaque or inlays (Fig. 5, Pl. 15*c–d*). But Face A is in fact the natural outer surface of the tusk, which cannot be used in carving. Either this surface is cut off at the outset or remains as a 'crust' following the removing of flat blanks (see above). **I-76** belongs to the first category, partly sawn and partly prised away from a cut block (cf. Krzyszkowska 1992*a*, 26, pl. 1j). A smaller piece (probably left-over as a 'crust') is **I-77**, which was found above the phase VII floor in Area 36 (Fig. 6, Pl. 15*b*). **I-78** is a little harder to understand. One side (A) represents the natural outer surface of the tusk, with a few trial cuttings across it (Fig. 4, Pl. 15*f*). The other face (B, Pl. 15*g*) is completely unworked, but displays longitudinal ridges. In fact, this indicates that the outer surface has split away from the ivory beneath. Whether this was deliberate or occurred during deposition is not clear. The piece came to light with disturbed material over Room II, although maybe should be associated with the main deposit of workshop material in Room II. The last few segments (**I-79** to **I-83**) offer

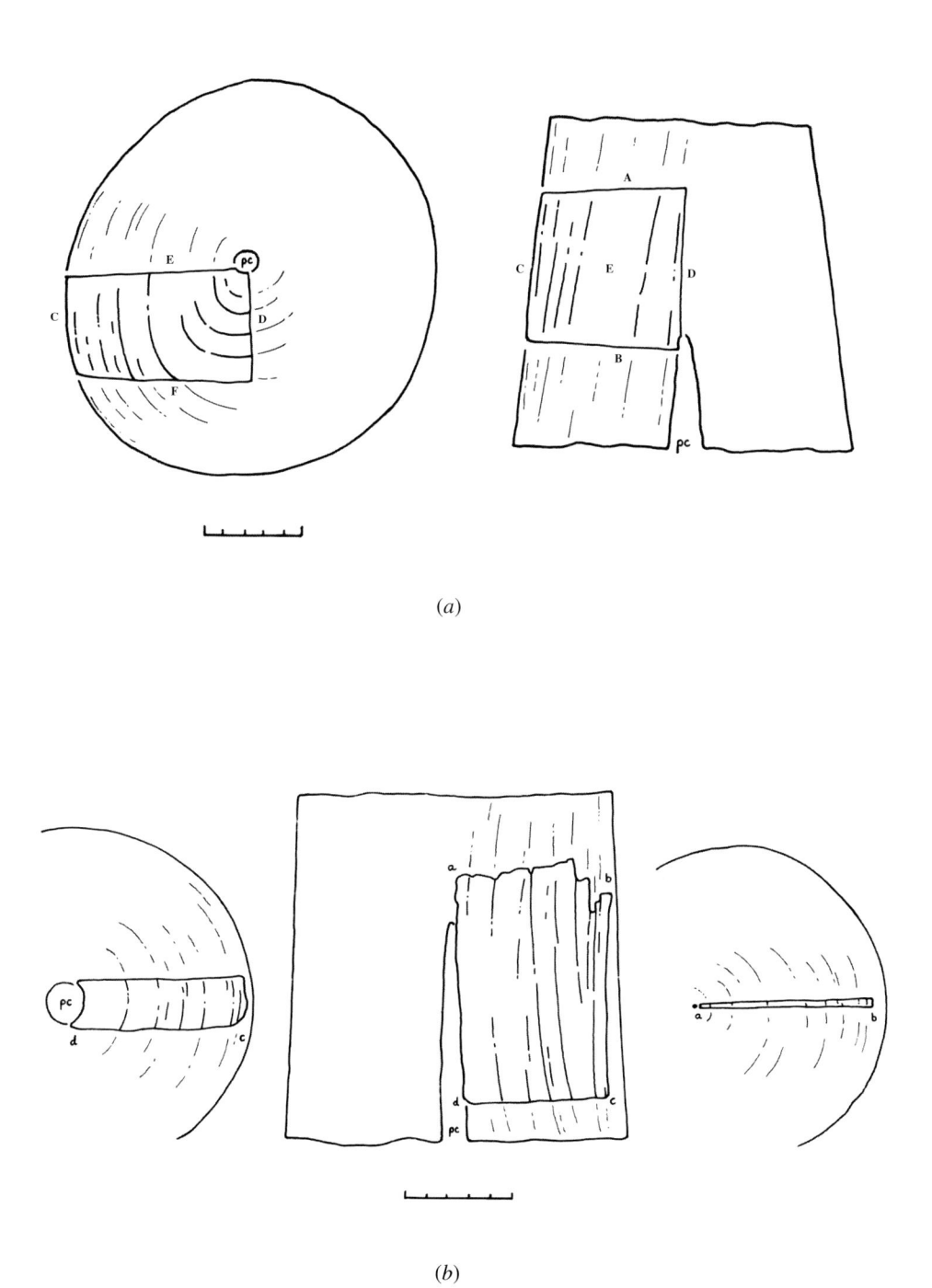

Fig. 9. Diagrams showing how (*a*) cube **I-70** and (*b*) wedge **I-73** were cut from tusk.

PLATE 14

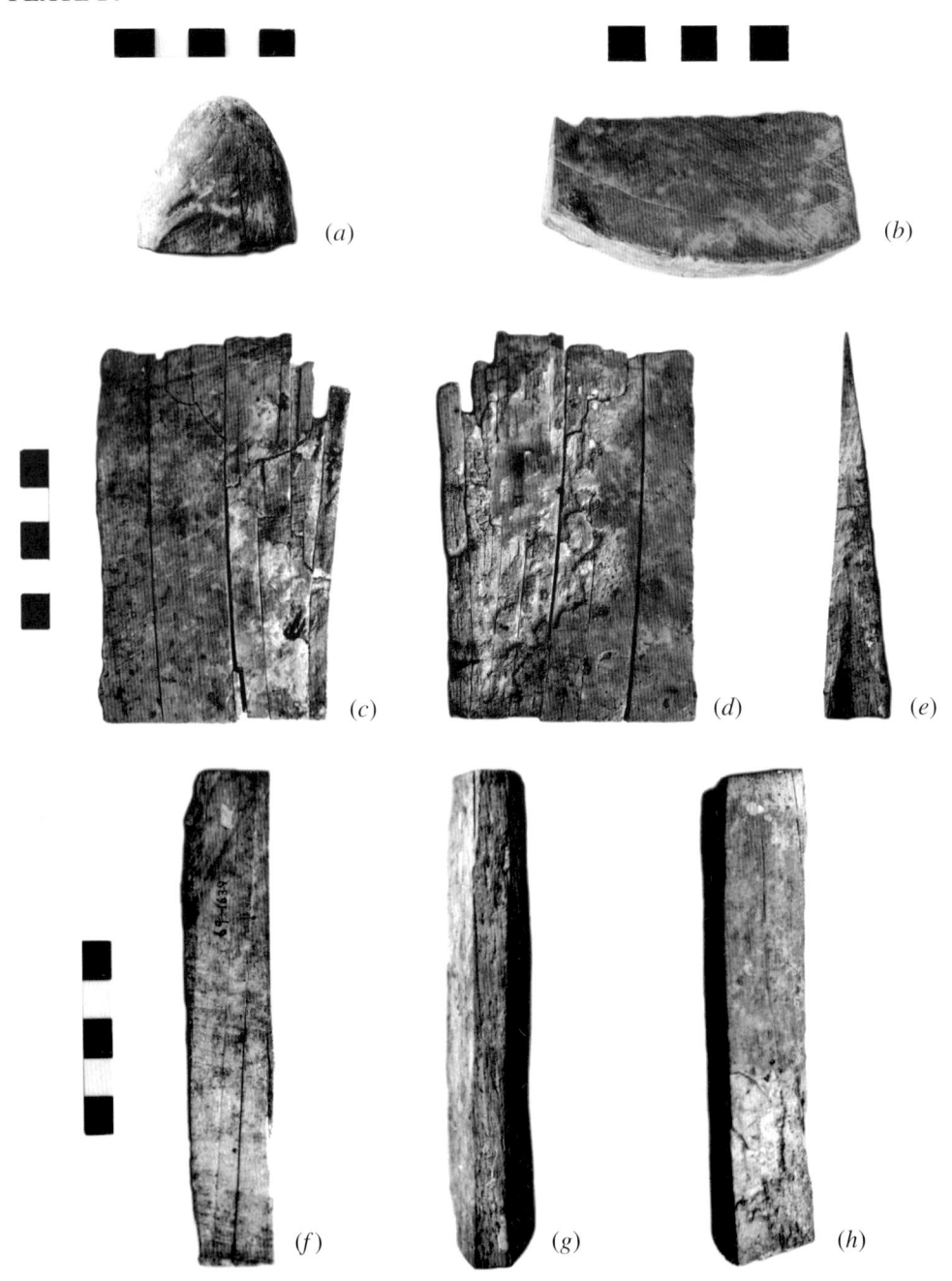

Partly worked ivories. Tusk tip: (*a*) **I-71** Face A. Large off-cuts: (*b*) **I-72** Face A; (*c*) **I-73** Face A; (*d*) **I-73** Face B; (*e*) **I-73** edge a–d with pulp cavity; (*f*) **I-74** Face A; (*g*) **I-74** Face B; (*h*) **I-74** Face C outer surface.

PLATE 15

Partly worked ivories. Off-cuts: (*a*) **I-75**; (*b*) **I-77**; (*c*) **I-76** Face A; (*d*) **I-76** Face B; (*e*) **I-79**; (*f*) **I-78** Face A; (*g*) **I-78** Face B; (*h*) **I-80**.

few insights, although **I-79** (Fig. 8, Pl. 15*e*) shows traces of a ridged or serrated tool similar to that used on comb blank (**I-69**). All are best seen as small off-cuts and are probably strays from Room 32. **I-80** came from Room 31; the others were scattered throughout the area but in association with phase IX and X material (see above pp. 14–16; Fig. 8).

Hippopotamus lower canine

All the partly worked ivory and virtually all of the finished products come from elephant tusk. This is not particularly surprising, for by the late Mycenaean period it was firmly established as the 'material of choice' among carvers and their clientele. Elephant ivory is not inherently better than hippopotamus ivory, but the tusks are undoubtedly more versatile. Against this backdrop, the large segment of hippopotamus tusk (**I-84**) represents an important discovery (Pl. 16). Indeed until correctly identified in 1978, there was no evidence whatsoever that hippopotamus ivory was used in the Aegean during the Bronze Age (Krzyszkowska 1984). Now the role of hippopotamus ivory in the Aegean is well documented, especially in Minoan Crete where it helped shape the character of the local industry from pre-palatial times until LM I. (Krzyszkowska 1988). It was also employed on the mainland from the Shaft Grave period onwards, while during LH/LM IIIA it appears to have been *de rigueur* for warrior head appliqués (Krzyszkowska 1991). Considerable progress has also been made in understanding its importance in the eastern Mediterranean and Egypt (Caubet and Poplin 1987; 1992; Krzyszkowska and Morkot 2000).

Our tusk, **I-84**, represents approximately one-quarter of a large lower canine. The segment comes from the distal end of a tusk, preserving the natural wear facet at one end, and is roughly broken at the other. In addition the piece has split lengthwise along the commissure, a natural fracture line peculiar to lower canines (Krzyszkowska 1990, 42–5, figs. 17–18, pls. 12–13). As preserved, the tusk shows no signs of working. Moreover, exposed surfaces are burnt and calcined, although in patches the ivory beneath remains whitish and appears 'fresh'.

The condition of the tusk is somewhat puzzling. It was found in the basement Room II of the Megaron complex, near a fragmentary block with spiral decoration (*WBM* 27, 23, fig. 13, cat. no. 50). These had apparently fallen into the room from above as a result of the phase VIII destruction. If so, it would help to explain why the tusk was burnt, whereas ivories from nearby are not. But this poses further problems: where had the tusk been kept before the destruction and what connection, if any, did it have to the other 'workshop material' just discussed. Although two of the inlays in Room 32 (**I-33** and **I-34**) may be made of hippopotamus ivory, there is no particular reason to link them to **I-84**.

Since the identification of **I-84** as a hippopotamus lower canine, another tusk from Mycenae has come to light. It was discovered by Dr Katie Demakopoulou among the Tsountas ivories, now stored in the National Museum (see below). The tusk is complete but has had some preliminary work done to it (Demakopoulou and Krzyszkowska in preparation). A third tusk, apparently unworked, is now attested at Thebes (Aravantinos 2000, 72–3, fig. 46). Numerous unworked tusks — lower canines and incisors — have also been recovered from the Uluburun wreck, along with a large cut segment of elephant tusk (Bass 1987, 726 colour photograph).

PLATE 16

Segment of hippopotamus tusk **I-84**.

WORKSHOPS AND WORKSHOP MATERIAL

As already noted, pieces of partly worked ivory were found by Schliemann on the acropolis. Overall, the range of material is comparable to ours, including large and small off-cuts, as well as a small cube similar to **I-70** (Poursat 1977*b*, cat. no. 19, pl. III illustrates the larger pieces; also Krzyszkowska 1992*a*, pls. 1c–d). Unfortunately we do not know where this material was discovered. Indeed it is not even certain that all the pieces now registered as NM 1022 came from the same area.[4] If anything, the ivories found by Tsountas have fared even worse. Although some appear in Poursat's catalogue (1977*b*, cat. nos. 20–48, pls. I–IV), many more languished in the basements of the National Museum, unregistered until 1971. The material has never been studied systematically, although the amount of information to be gained may be limited.[5] Certainly, there are pieces of partly worked ivory comparable to ours (Sakellarakis 1979, fig. 48 shows a selection only; scale not stated is *c*. 2:3). There is even a hippopotamus tusk (see above; Demakopoulou and Krzyszkowska in preparation). Are there also left-overs and pieces of salvage? These would be extremely hard to recognize among pieces that are ostensibly finished, without associated material to guide us.

The lack of information concerning the Schliemann and Tsountas ivories is a major blow, since individually and collectively they offer the best comparanda for our material. The finds from the Artisans' Quarter, excavated by Mylonas, are harder to assess from the brief preliminary report and single photograph (Mylonas 1966, 425 pl. 96a; cf. Tournavitou 1995, 192–3). The pieces of ivory *seem* to be small, fairly regular off-cuts and trimmings, perhaps from inlay manufacture. But since no scale is provided, this impression may be false. Glass, gold leaf and pieces of semi-precious stones were also reported. But it is far from clear whether we are dealing with an actual working area or storerooms for a workshop. Much better known is the material from the 'Ivory Houses' outside the Citadel. But these contained few examples of partly worked ivory (Krzyszkowska 1992*a*, 32 n. 26). Among the numerous inlays, however, are good examples of mistakes and possible rejects (e.g. Tournavitou 1995, pl. 18), supporting the idea that these were made in large job-lots and used as required. It would appear that Poursat's interpretation of the houses is substantially correct, namely that they represent 'une sorte d'entrepôt, … où l'on adaptait les ivoires aux meubles qu'ils devaient décorer' (1977*a*, 136). It is also possible that some ivories were salvaged from furniture that had been damaged and dismantled. In any case, it is clear that the 'Ivory Houses' do not offer a good parallel for our collection. This is all the more unfortunate since they were destroyed during LH IIIB, probably contemporary with our phase VII.

Further afield pieces of partly worked ivory occur mostly as singletons or as strays (e.g. Nichoria, Pylos, Tiryns: Krzyszkowska 1992*a*; 2002, 191–2, 194–6). Thebes is a notable exception, but the ivory 'workshop material' found in various parts of the Kadmeion has yet to be published.[6] The much earlier material from the Royal Road at Knossos displays somewhat different features — *not* because it is earlier, but because the end-products were different (*pace* Tournavitou 1997). Indeed the Royal Road provides our best collection of *débitage*, indicating the presence of an ivory workshop proper. But whereas this material (probably waste from carving in the round) is exclusively elephant ivory, the hundreds of finished inlays (?already assembled on boxes) are made from hippopotamus ivory (Krzyszkowska 1988; 1992*a*).

Though this survey may seem disappointing, it does help to put our collection in perspective. It is perfectly clear that we do not have an ivory workshop *per se* within the confines of the site as excavated. There is no *débitage* to speak of and barely a handful of objects came from the partially open Area 36. Most of the workshop material — including possible unused inlays and salvage — was concentrated in two areas: basement Room II in the Megaron complex and Room 32 in the Room with the Fresco Complex. With the exception of the comb blank (**I-69**), the strays in later contexts can almost certainly be associated with these two deposits. Room II was apparently a storeroom; Room 32 may have been a storeroom-cum-shrine since it contained the wheelmade figure 69-1221. In any case, Room 32 belongs to the Room with the Fresco Complex, one of several cult areas on the southwestern slope. By contrast the function of the Megaron within the Cult Centre remains uncertain.

But how to explain the presence of our 'workshop material' in these areas? First we need to remember that the amount of primary raw material is minimal. The prepared block (**I-70**) and *possibly* the piece of hippopotamus tusk (**I-84**) are the sole exceptions. The handful of blanks could also be turned into finished objects. The inlays were usable at a push, but it is doubtful that any amount of work would turn our large unfinished pieces into serviceable objects. The best hope was that they might yield ivory for secondary manufacture. The same applies to the large off-cuts. The hilt-plates and other pieces of salvage faced an uncertain future. The waste pieces have no value whatsoever. In short, it is virtually impossible to interpret our material as ivory stored *for use* in a workshop.

This is not to deny that the material had originated in a workshop — its very nature makes that clear. But why rubbish of this kind should be saved and stored remains a mystery. Our best clues come from Room 32, since its role in cult is assured. It may be that the material here was dedicated by a workshop, or less plausibly, by individual craftsmen. Parallels do exist for workshop debris or unfinished pieces being dedicated in shrines. A misshapen glass seal came to light in Room 19, as well as a glass plaque that may have been unfinished (*WBM* 10, 111).[7] Debris of various sorts was also found in the sanctuary at Phylakopi (Renfrew 1985, 387–9). This is not to say that the Room with the Fresco Complex exercised direct control over an ivory workshop. The evidence is too slender for that. Moreover, the ivories in basement Room II of the Megaron also need explaining. Whatever link existed between cult and craft in the Citadel House Area, its nature still remains stubbornly elusive (Krzyszkowska 1997).

PART 2. OBJECTS OF BONE, ANTLER AND BOAR'S TUSK

This part deals with 109 catalogued entries, representing 115 individual items of bone, horn, antler and boar's tusk. By far the largest number of objects (75) are bone, e.g. handles, pins, tools and partly worked segments. Antler accounts for a further 17 items, mostly tools. Finished objects made of boar's tusk are few, but also included in the catalogue are unworked tusks, perhaps intended for use (below). Additionally, 14 pieces of unworked bone, 13 of which were originally inventoried as small finds, but are not artifacts, are catalogued under (**U**) (see pp. 456–69).

CATEGORIES

The items considered here fall naturally into four groups, based on their material, i.e. bone, horn, antler and boar's tusk. As with the ivories presented in Part 1, finished form and degree of modification to the raw material provide criteria for classification. The largest group (bone) has the most variation. Items range from finely worked pins, needles and 'spatulae' — where the natural features of the raw material have been largely obliterated — to utilitarian tools made from segments of long bones or ribs, modified only slightly. Casual points like these can be found on almost any site of any period, though precise parallels are often hard to find. However, in the past, bone tools were probably overlooked at rich LBA palace sites; the same would surely apply to partly worked segments. By contrast, close comparisons exist at Mycenae itself and further afield for our pins, needles and the enigmatic 'spatulae'. Among the examples of partly worked bone are two unfinished pins and various waste segments. Whether the worked horn core is also waste or represents raw material stored at the time of the catastrophe cannot now be determined (see below pp. 55–6, 72).

The use of antler in the LBA is not well attested, at least in published sources. Indeed one could argue that antler has fared even worse than bone, since the material itself is sometimes misidentified (see below pp. 54, 73). The pointed tools from the Citadel House Area form an exceptionally interesting group, while the fine handle and pin are also noteworthy.

The principal use of boar's tusk in the LBA Aegean was for helmet plates. Only four plates — all clearly strays — were found in the Citadel House Area. However, the concentration of 13 unworked tusks in Room II suggests that these may have been stored for use. Although the same need not apply to every unworked tusk found on the site, all examples have been catalogued for sake of completeness.

As remarked in Part 1, it is no easy matter to devise a coherent typology for a small disparate collection. Thus the categories below should be regarded as broad headings only, intended to facilitate discussion and comparisons. A letter prefix indicates the material from which the item is made; cases of uncertainty are indicated (e.g. **B/I** or **A/B**) with further explanation in text or on the CD.

BONE
- **B/I-1 to B-3** Handles for bronze implements.
- **B-4 to B-27** **Pins and needles**. This category can be further sub-divided according to the shape of heads (e.g. plain, bulbous, groove and torus decoration, pierced). For undiagnostic fragments see below **B-33** to **B-46**.
- **B-28 to B-32** **'Spatulae'**. Pin-like objects with one end spatulate in shape.
- **B-33 to B-46** **Undiagnostic fragments** of pins, needles or 'spatulae'.
- **B-47 to B-51** **Miscellaneous**.
- **B-52 to B-66** **Tools** made from pointed segments of long bones or ribs.
- **B-67 to B-75** **Partly worked bone**, including unfinished items and waste segments.

HORN
- **H-1** Worked horn core

ANTLER
- **A-1** **Handle** for a bronze implement.
- **A/B-2** **Pin** with decorated head.
- **A-3 to A-15** **Tools**, usually made from long segments of main beam.
- **A-16 to A-17** **Partly worked segments**

BOAR'S TUSK
- **BT-1 to BT-4** Helmet plates
- **BT-5 to BT-16** Unworked tusks

MATERIALS

In living animals bone (the material) and bones (the anatomical parts) have specific functions and, by extension, specific characteristics. The same is equally true for antler (a related osseous material), boar's tusk (consisting of dentine covered by enamel) and ivory. The characteristics — morphology, surface features, structure — helped determine choice of material for particular end-products in antiquity. These matters are discussed in the appropriate sections, below. The same characteristics also help us to identify the materials today (Krzyszkowska 1990). In our collection diagnostic features were absent only in a few cases (e.g. the knife handles **B/I-1** and **B/I-2** and the pin **A/B-2**). Unfortunately ivory and related materials are not always identified accurately in published sources. For example pins — ordinarily made of bone — are all too often described as 'ivory'. Antler is sometimes mistaken for bone or is misleadingly termed 'horn', particularly in American literature. In reality, antlers are the bony outgrowths from the skulls of male deer, which are grown and shed annually (Krzyszkowska 1990, 58–64). By contrast horns are carried permanently by sheep, goat and cattle. They consist of a bony core covered by a sheath of keratinous material, also found in claws and hooves. It is this tough and pliable material (i.e. horn) which is worked, not the bony core. Although the bony cores survive in the Aegean, the actual horn does not (Krzyszkowska 1990, 92–3, pl. 31).

Unlike ivory, which had to be imported (above p. 4), all of the materials considered here could be obtained as by-products from husbandry and hunting of indigenous species, i.e. domesticated sheep/goat, pigs, cattle; wild boar and red deer. Unfortunately few systematic studies of faunal material have been undertaken for Mycenaean sites. Thus our ability to correlate the use of the raw materials and the exploitation of these species for food (or sport) is limited.[8]

FIND CONTEXTS AND CHRONOLOGY

As noted in Part 1 most of the ivories were concentrated in deposits dating to phases VII and VIII. By contrast objects of bone, antler and boar's tusk have a much wider chronological spread, distributed throughout phases VII–XI. In addition a few pieces pre-date the main phase VI construction, while a handful derive from the Hellenistic period (XIV). There are few significant concentrations of material, although further insights may be possible when associated finds are fully published.

EARLY CONTEXTS

Three items pre-date the main LH IIIB construction. One tool (**B-52**) was found beneath Passage 34 with Neo–LH II pottery (phase IV and below), another (**B-53**) came from fill below the Small Courtyard. A helmet plate (**BT-1**) was found in LH IIIA levels over the cemetery area and could well be a stray from one of the graves. Several more items belong to the main LH IIIB construction phase. They include tools **B-54** (from below Room 12) and **B-55** (from W of the cemetery area), as well as helmet plate **BT-2** and unworked tusk **BT-6** (both from beneath the floor of Area 36). In addition, a plain pin (**B-4**) came to light in Room 14, while a segment of partly worked antler (**A-16**) was found in or below Room 15. Fig. 10 illustrates selected pieces.

PHASE VII (CATASTROPHE DURING LH IIIB)

In this phase we find several important groups of objects recovered from rooms which also contained notable concentrations of ivories.

Room II

Room II contained 13 unworked boar's tusks (**BT-8** to **BT-14**, Pl. 21) in addition to the numerous ivory inlays (some probably unused) and partly worked ivory (above p. 6). It is therefore likely that the tusks had been collected and stored pending manufacture, although doubts have been expressed as to whether boar's tusk helmets were actually made after the Early Mycenaean period (below pp. 76–7). A single finished helmet plate was also found in Room II (**BT-3**, Pl. 21). Another interesting find is the 'spatula' (**B-28**, Fig. 11, Pl. 18); two more of these enigmatic objects were recovered in phase VIII contexts (**B-29** and **B-30**, below).

Room 32

Room 32, where much partly worked ivory was found, also contained horn core **H-1** (Fig. 11, Pl. 19). It is possible that the bony core was still covered with horn (i.e. the keratinous sheath) at the time of the catastrophe. If so, then we are dealing with another kind of raw material in store. But if the horn had already been removed for use, then the core — consisting of very cancellous (spongy) bone — would have been waste. Also found in Room 32 were two pointed

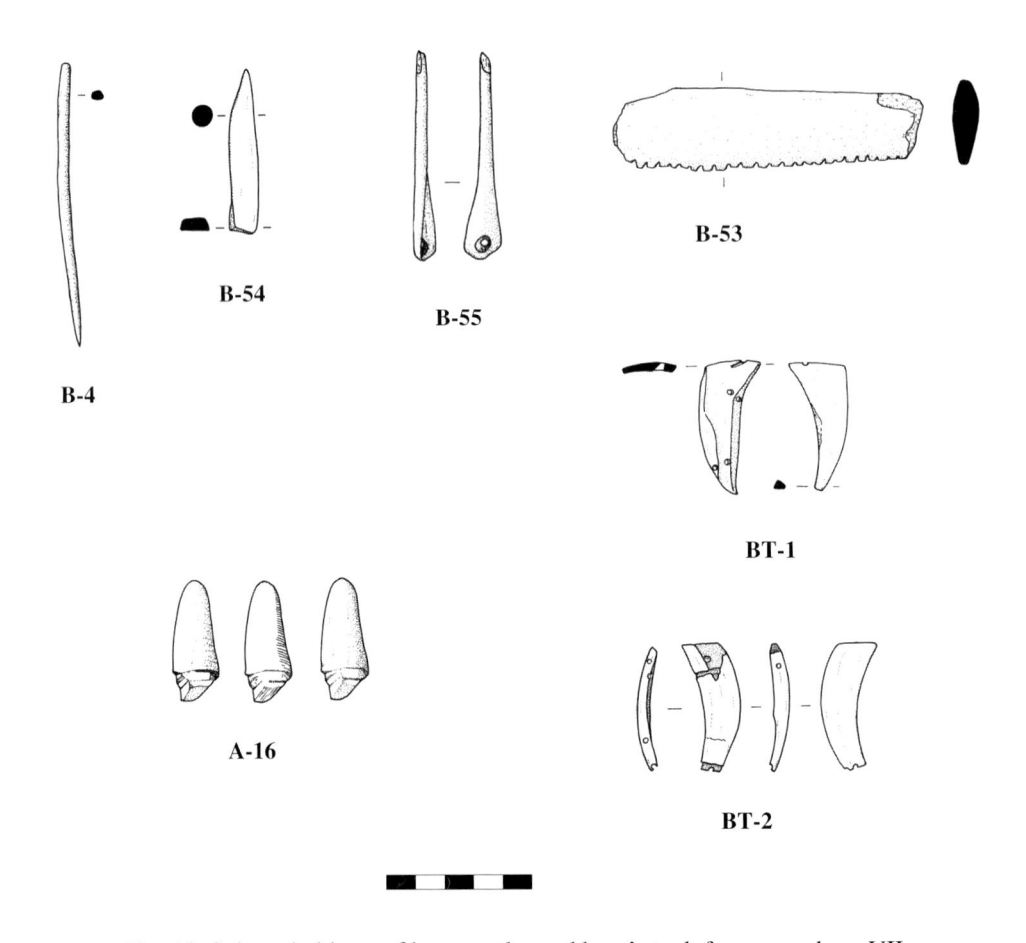

Fig. 10. Selected objects of bone, antler and boar's tusk from pre-phase VII.

tools made of antler (**A-3** and **A-4**, Fig. 11, Pl. 20). The first belongs to the main phase VII floor deposit, while **A-4** was found at the interface of the floor deposit and the back filling of this area at the beginning of phase VIII. The same applies to a third example (**A-5**) found in Room 31, though it may be even earlier. All three were probably in store in Room 32 during phase VII. Another stray in Room 31 is tool **B-56** (Fig. 11).

Area 36
Area 36, which is adjacent to the Room with the Fresco Complex, yielded five more antler tools (**A-6** to **A-9** directly on 'floor 2' and **A-10** just above the floor. Fig. 11, Pl. 20). As already noted, a few inlays and examples of partly worked ivory also provide a link between the two areas (above p. 9). The antler tools form a distinctive and homogeneous group, although their precise function has yet to be determined. They generally have rather blunt points, with wear patterns apparently caused by rubbing or polishing. A role in jewellery manufacture is possible (below pp. 74–6). A fine steatite mould for gold and glass ornaments was recovered in Area 36 (*WBM* 27, 29–31)

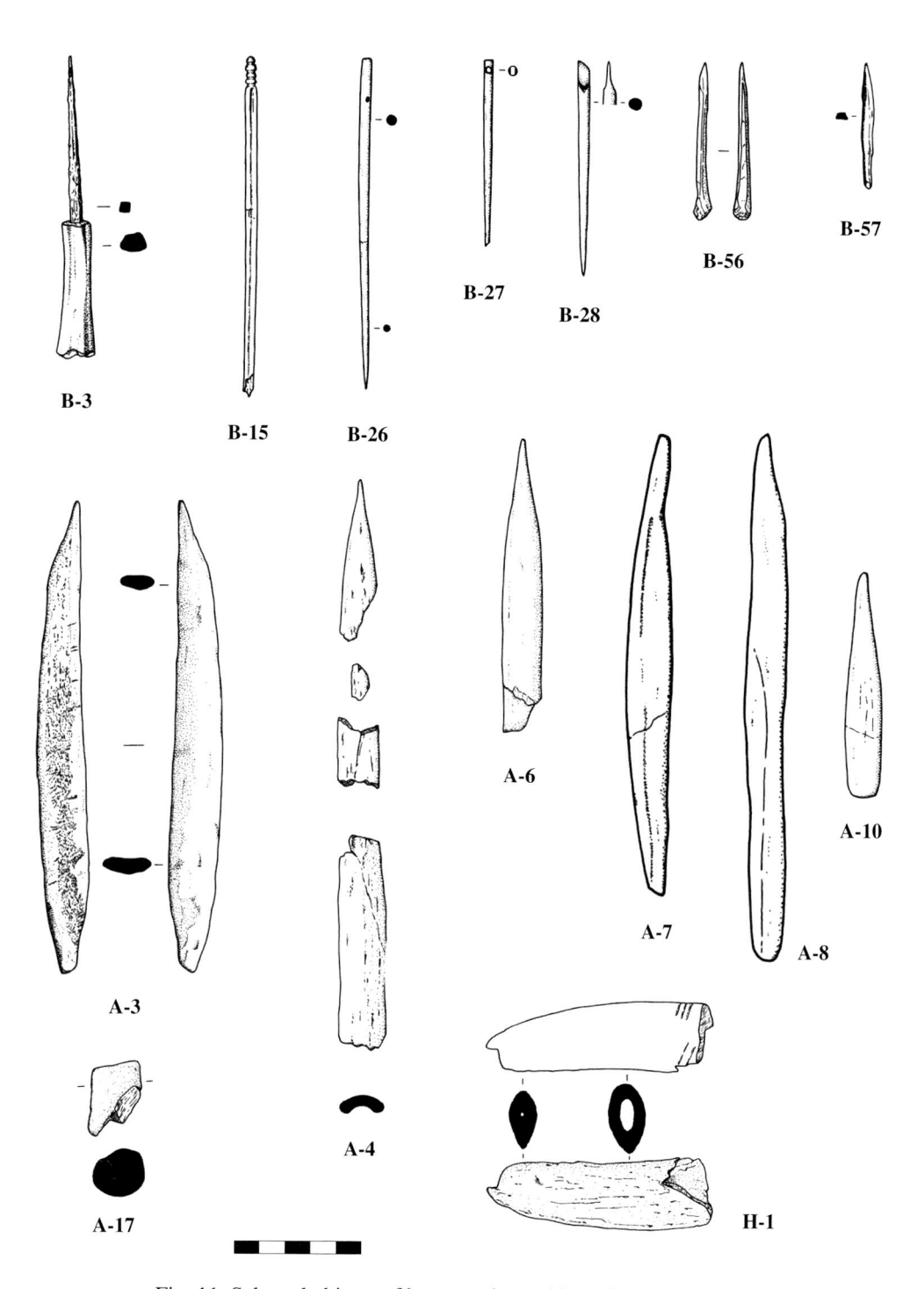

Fig. 11. Selected objects of bone, antler and horn from phase VII.

as were two glass ornaments, though these were not made in this mould. The absence of waste, however, makes it unlikely that glass was being worked here. The presence of glass items spoilt during manufacture in Rooms 11 and 14 does support the view that cast glass objects were produced somewhere near the site (H. Hughes-Brock, *WBM* 25 forthcoming).

Other finds from Area 36 (Fig. 11) include an exceptionally well preserved bronze awl, mounted in a bone handle (**B-3**), a fine needle (**B-27**) and a slender pointed tool, which may have been hafted (**B-57**). All could have been used in working leather or cloth. A pin with a ribbed head (**B-15**) may also may belong to the phase VII floor in this area and, if so, represents the only intact decorated pin from LH IIIB levels. This is in marked contrast to the many fine pins recovered from LH IIIC contexts. However, two small pin/needle fragments were found with phase VII material in Rooms xxiv and 32 (**B-33** and **B-34**).

Room 18
A fine needle (**B-26**, Fig. 11) recovered during the removal of the phase VIII floor must belong to phase VII use of the room. The same probably applies to a partly worked antler tine (**A-17**, Fig. 11) found in the Alcove of Room 18. No items of bone, antler or boar's tusk were recovered in Room 19: two pieces of bone, which were originally inventoried as artifacts 68-1506 and 68-1508 (*WBM* 10, 18, 174), prove to be unworked, see pp. 456–7.

PHASE VIII (DESTRUCTION AT THE END OF LH IIIB2)
About a dozen objects of bone were recovered from phase VIII contexts, scattered across the site (see Fig. 12 for selected pieces). A bronze knife with bone or ivory handle (**B/I-1**) came from the floor deposit in South House Annex Room 7, which also contained a few ivories (above p. 14). A 'spatula' was found nearby in Room 5 (**B-29**) another came from the floor deposit in Room 1 (**B-30**). A plain pin (**B-5**) was found outside Room 38, while a small fragment of a pin or needle belongs to the phase VIII floor deposit in Room XI of the Temple Complex (**B-37**). This is probably nothing more than a stray, as are similar fragments found with mixed phase VII and VIII debris over Room II (**B-35**) and in Room 3 (**B-36**). Five bone tools are also surely strays. One (**B-58**) came from the deliberate infill in Room 32; another (**B-59**) was found with collapsed material in Room 18; while three more (**B-60**, **B-61**, **B-62**) came from Passage 34, also associated with collapsed debris or later levelling. The phase VIII floor in this passage yielded a curious example of partly worked bone (**B-67**). Finally, a bone button (**B-47**) was recovered with disturbed material in Room 4. Aside from the bronze knife (**B/I-1**) and the two 'spatulae' (**B-29** and **B-30**) the phase VIII finds are disappointing (cf. p. 12).

PHASE IX (EARLY LH IIIC)
Only nine objects made from bone and antler come from Phase IX contexts. Some items could well be earlier products displaced following the LH IIIB destructions (phases VII and VIII) or disturbed in later terracing. This explanation seemed to account for the presence of some ivories, including 'workshop material' in phase IX contexts (above p. 14). Unfortunately, objects of bone and antler are harder to date, especially when comparanda are lacking. This is true of the fine handle with incised decoration (**A-1**, Fig. 13, Pl. 17) found in cleaning. Two antler tools (Fig. 13) may well belong with the main phase VII group (above), although they differ in shape.

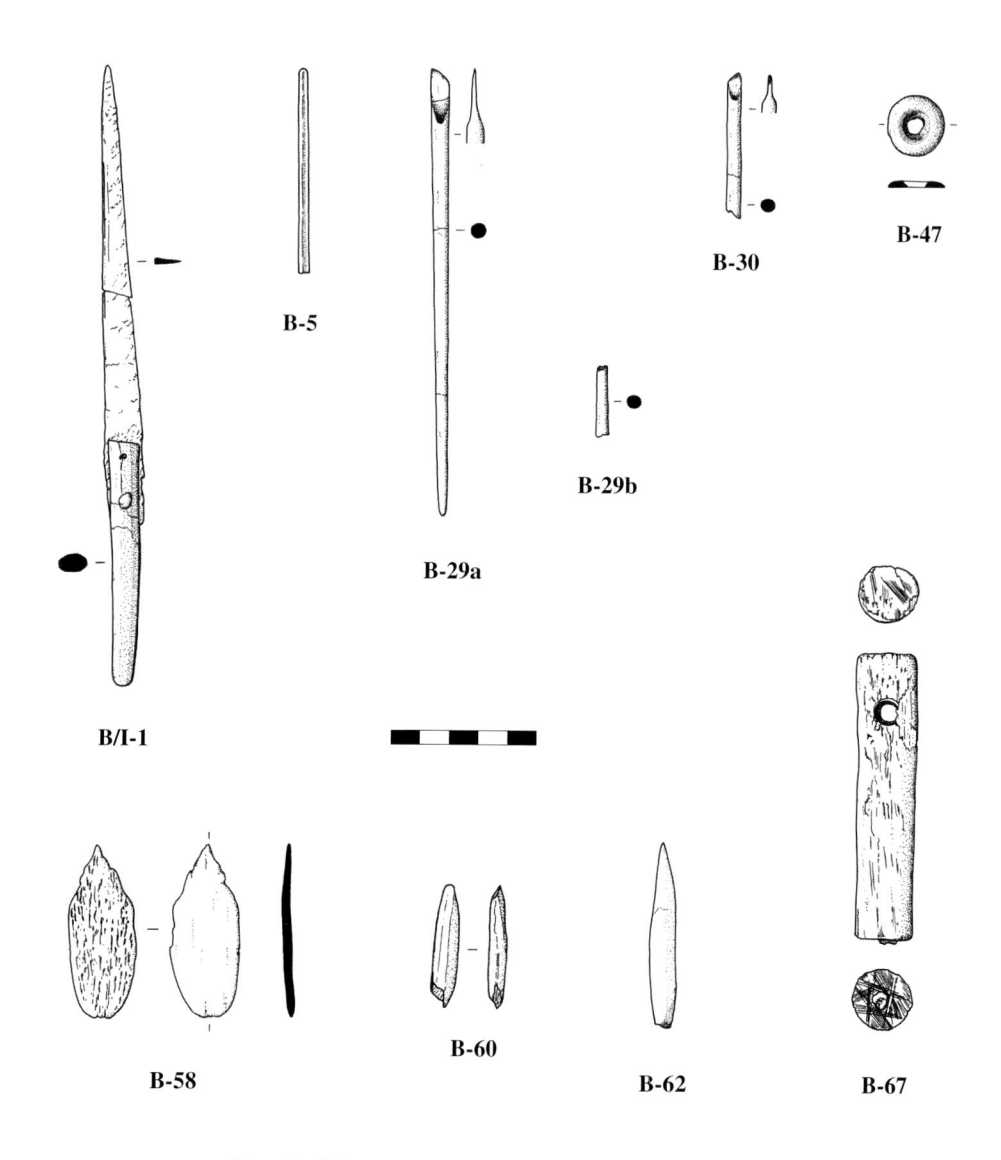

Fig. 12. Selected objects of bone from phase VIII.

One (**A-11**) was found during cleaning of walls ac/ab (i.e. Room xxi); another (**A-12**) came from Room xxxiii. Two more items found beneath phase IX floors may well be earlier strays: a pin fragment (**B-38**) from below Room xxxi and a waste segment of bone (**B-70**, Fig. 13) from the area over Room 31. By far the most interesting item associated with phase IX is an unfinished pin (**B-68**, Fig. 13, Pl. 19) found in the upper level of Room xxi. There is no good reason to doubt that this was made in LH IIIC; another unfinished pin (**B-69**) comes from phase X (see below). On the floor in Room xxi was a grooved object, perhaps a broken pinhead (**B-48**, Fig.

13), while a very fine pin with ribbed head (**B-16**) was found with collapsed material overlying Room 31. Finally, the floor deposit in Room xxxiv yielded a small fragment of unworked tusk from a boar or a pig (**BT-15**).

PHASE X (EARLY–TOWER PHASES OF LH IIIC)
Seventeen items of bone, antler and boar's tusk come from phase X contexts (see Fig. 13 for a selection). The first, a bronze knife with traces of bone (or perhaps ivory) adhering to the rivets (**B/I-2**) came from beneath the floor in Room liii; it may well be an earlier product. Only one object, an unfinished pin (**B-69**, Fig. 13, Pl. 19) from Room liii, was clearly associated with a floor deposit. Also found in the same room were a pin fragment (**B-41**) and a piece of partly worked bone (**B-71**). These and indeed most other items associated with phase X came to light in disturbed material, e.g. resulting from initial collapse of earth and mud-brick, upper fill, or later collapse and wash levels (see CD-ROM for details). The finest objects are the pins: two with bulbous heads (**B-11** and **B-12**, Pl. 18), two with ribbed heads (**B-17** (Pl. 18) and **A/B-2**) and three fragments (**B-39**, **B-40**; **B-41** mentioned above). The three bone tools from phase X are uninformative (**B-63**, **B-64**, **B-65**). Two segments of partly worked bone (**B-72** and **B-73**) recovered in the upper fill over Room xxx are more interesting. The pieces compare closely in size and shape, though it is impossible to judge whether they are waste from earlier processes or blanks abandoned during manufacture. Finally, a small portion of unworked boar's tusk (**BT-16**) came from below the Tower.

PHASE XI (ADVANCED AND DEVELOPED PHASES OF LH IIIC)
Nine objects of bone, all pins, came to light in Phase XI contexts (see Fig. 13 and Pl. 18 for a selection). Once again, all were associated with collapsed material and wash levels. The pins include four with plain heads (**B-6** to **B-10**), one with a slightly bulbous head (**B-13**) and three with finely ribbed heads (**B-18** to **B-20**). No items of antler or boar's tusk were recovered.

PHASE XII (WASH LEVELS AND GRAVES, FINAL LH IIIC, SUB-MYCENAEAN, PG)
Two bone pins (**B-21** and **B-22**, Pl. 18) were found in the vicinity of the SM/PG graves. Both have finely decorated heads, which seem to have been damaged and re-worked. One other item, a curious ?spoon (**B-49**, Fig. 13), perhaps belongs to this phase, although it was found in collapse and wash levels, which also contained phase XI material. No objects of antler or boar's tusk were recovered.

PHASE XIV (HELLENISTIC)
From the Hellenistic occupation of the site came a handful of bone objects (Fig. 14). There is a fine pin with ribbed head (**B-25**) and two pin fragments (**B-43**, **B-44**); two possible styli (**B-31** and **B-32**); and a worn button or bead (**B-51**). A segment of partly worked bone (**B-74**) was also found below the yard floor. The antler tool (**A-13**, Fig. 14) is puzzling. Although this came from floor levels in yard HH, one wonders if it is truly a Hellenistic product (see also below p. 76).

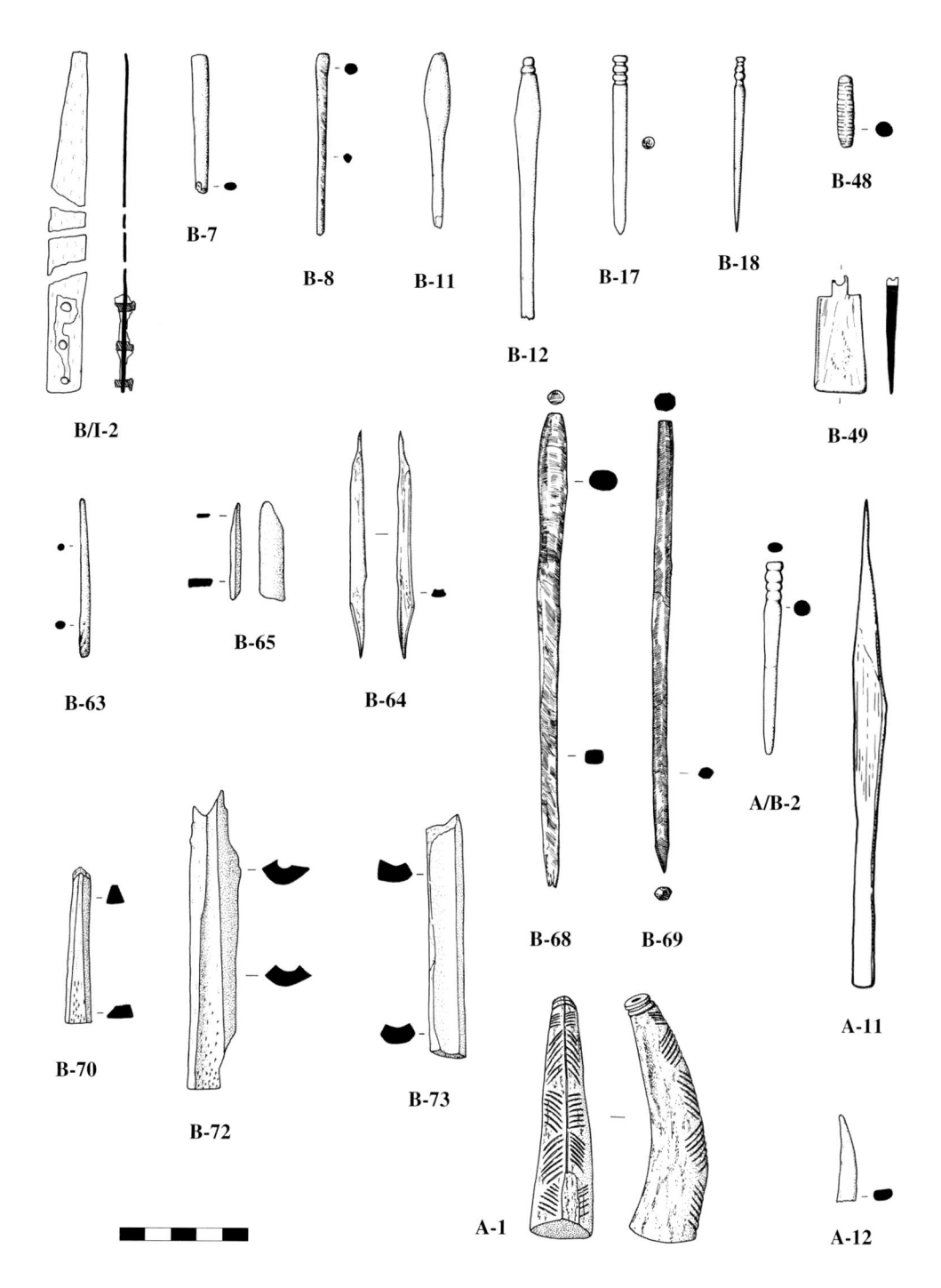

Fig. 13. Selected objects of bone and antler from phases IX, X and XI.

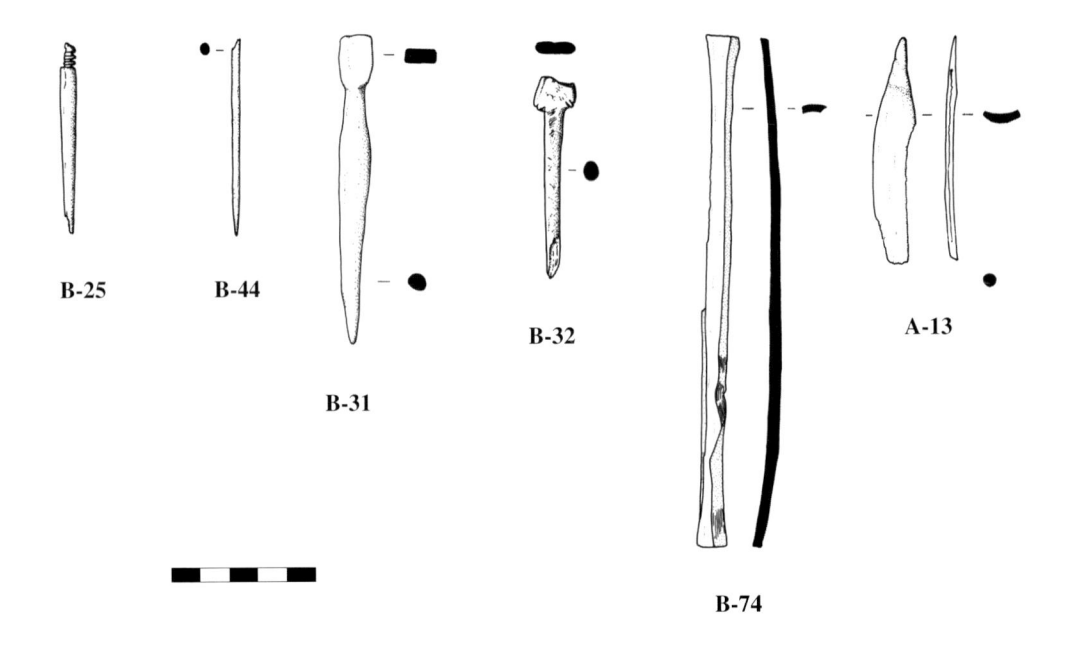

Fig. 14. Selected objects of bone and antler from phase XIV (Hellenistic).

MIXED AND SURFACE LEVELS

Seven objects were associated with material of mixed (LBA/Hellenistic) date, while a further five came from year-surface levels (see selection in Fig. 15). Individually most are unexciting and virtually impossible to date. These include the pins (**B-14**, **B-23**, **B-24**), pin fragments (**B-42**, **B-45**, **B-46**), broken ?pinhead (**B-50**), tool (**B-66**) and waste segment (**B-75**). However, the helmet plate (**BT-4**) is surely a LBA product and the same may well be true of the broken fragments of antler tools (**A-14** and **A-15**).

THE OBJECTS

In this section we consider specific objects of bone, antler and boar's tusk in greater detail. The main categories have already been outlined above (p. 54); discussion generally follows the catalogue order. It must be admitted that some individual items are of little interest (e.g. pin fragments). Our attention will focus on those groups which contribute most to our understanding of how bone, antler and boar's tusk were exploited during the Mycenaean period.

BONE

During the Bronze Age bone was a readily available by-product of animal husbandry. The long bones of sheep/goat and cattle were most frequently used, since they offered significant amounts of compact bone and possessed good tensile strength (Krzyszkowska 1990, 53–8, figs. 21–3, pl.

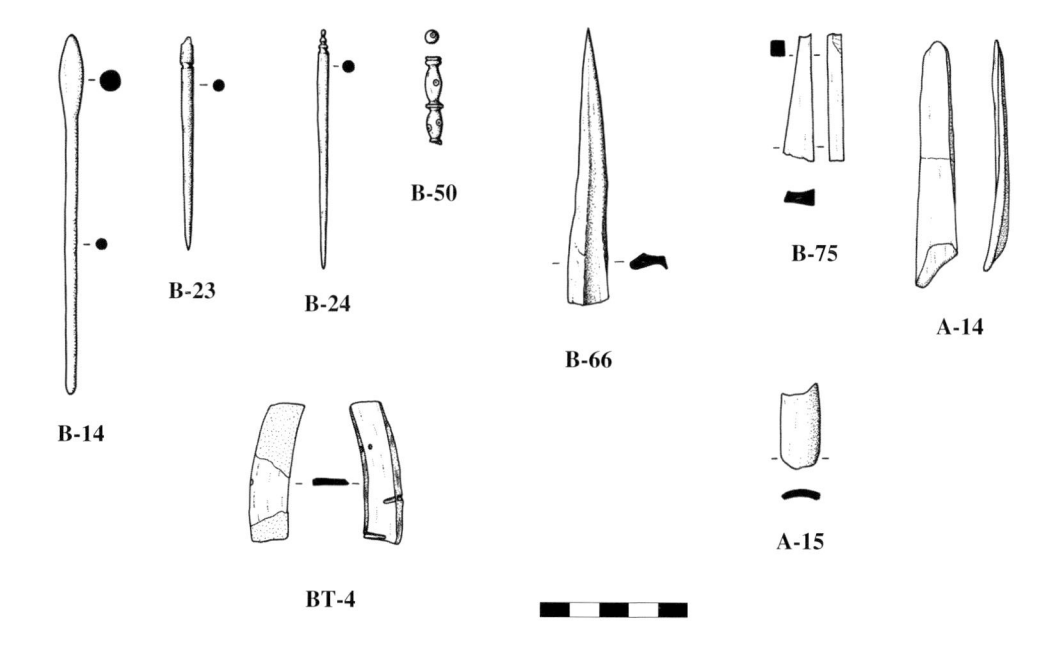

Fig. 15. Selected objects of bone, antler and boar's tusk from mixed and surface levels.

21). This is particularly true of the metapodials (bones of the feet), which have thick, straight shafts and have little nutritional value (cooked bone being unsuitable for working). Thus they were ideal for making pins or needles and were also suitable for small decorative objects (e.g. buttons, inlays etc.). Even on sites where ivory is common, bone is the material of choice for pin manufacture. This is certainly the case at Mycenae and other LBA Aegean sites. Splinters of long bones also make good tools, though rarely can we be certain of the precise bone or species when segments are heavily worked. Flat bones, especially cattle ribs, were frequently fashioned into tools during the EBA, though by the LBA this practice was rare. It remains unclear whether this reflects a change in butchery techniques or in the activities for which tools were required.

Handles

Two bronze knives from the site have handles made of bone or ivory (**B/I-1** and **B/I-2**, Figs. 12, 13, Pl. 17). Although the first is fairly well preserved, the material cannot be identified with certainty. There are no clear diagnostic signs that it is ivory, while both size and shape would be feasible in bone. Only amorphous traces of the second handle survive (Fig. 13). Published comparanda are few (see p. 304) and handles described as 'ivory' need to be confirmed by autopsy. Our third handle (**B-3**, Fig. 11, Pl. 17) belongs to an altogether different type and is made from a pig metapodial. The distal end of the bone with little modification served as the grip, the proximal end was cut off straight and into the marrow cavity was inserted a fine bronze awl. This type of handle is attested in the Aegean from the EBA onwards, though few examples retain their bronze tools *in situ* (see p. 308 for references). To my knowledge this is the sole example from a Mycenaean site, although a bronze chisel still in its antler handle was found at Tiryns (*Tiryns V*, 15, pl. 23.2–4).

Pins and needles

Twenty-four pins and needles made from bone were found in the Citadel House Area. In addition there are 15 fragments, which probably belonged to pins or needles, although 'spatulae' cannot be ruled out entirely (below pp. 67–9). Seven pins have plain heads, i.e. not set off from the shaft. One example (**B-4**, Fig. 10), found beneath the floor of Room 14, is complete (L. 0.095 m). All others (**B-5** to **B-10**) lack their pointed ends, but were probably about the same size. The unfinished example (**B-69**, Fig. 13, Pl. 19) would probably have reached L. 0.15 m after trimming.

The most interesting pins from the site are those with bulbous heads, where the shaft swells to its maximum diameter just below the top of the head (Fig. 13, Pl. 18). One example (**B-13**) is extremely slender and, with its very slight swelling, almost seems transitional between the plain and bulbous-headed varieties. A second (**B-14**) is also slender but has a more pronounced swelling, while **B-11** is an altogether sturdier example. A variation in the basic design occurs on **B-12**, where the bulbous element is surmounted by groove and torus decoration. One of the unfinished pins (**B-68**, Fig. 13, Pl. 19) was almost certainly destined to have a bulbous head; after trimming it would have been about L. 0.15 m.

The remaining pins have decorated heads, usually consisting of several grooves and toruses, best illustrated by the long example **B-15** (L. ex. 0.13 m) from Area 36 (Fig. 11). Very few pins were found in phase VII or VIII contexts on the site: this is the only one with a decorated head. There are subtle variations on the basic groove and torus design (see selection on Pl. 18). One example (**B-16**) has a mushroom-shaped element at the very top, a flat torus and a small inverted cone just above the neck. Another (**B-19**) has an inverted cone at the very top above four grooves and toruses of differing sizes. The ribbed head of **B-21** has a curious semi-circular section, probably the result of damage, which was then smoothed and polished. The head of **B-22**, now bi-conical, also seems to be re-worked. This example was found in a disturbed SM/PG grave, while **B-21** came to light near an adjacent grave. Re-working may also help explain why some examples seem unusually short and stubby (e.g. **B-18** and **B-20**, L. *c.* 0.065 m). Most Mycenaean pins, whether plain or decorated, fall within the range of L. 0.10–0.15 m, dimensions which can be comfortably achieved from cattle (or deer) metapodials.

Two bone needles were recovered from LH IIIB levels on the site (Fig. 11). The first (**B-26**) is unusual in having two tiny holes off-centre and at right angles to each other. The second (**B-27**, Pl. 18) is more conventional, with a flat head and small circular piercing. A third example made of ivory (**I-16**, Fig. 7) is broken, but preserves traces of its eye.

Few Mycenaean pins and needles have been adequately published. As already noted, there was a tendency in older literature to describe all non-utilitarian objects, including pins, as 'ivory'. But, in reality, few pins and even fewer needles are made of ivory: thus, our two examples (**I-15** and **I-16**) are noteworthy. Further confusion arises because the terms 'pins' and 'needles' are sometimes used interchangeably. Although many pins (and a few needles?) were found by Schliemann and Tsountas on the acropolis (Poursat 1977*b*, cat. nos. 18, 35, 38, pl. III), they have not been systematically studied, nor are many of their find-spots known. The re-use of tombs further hampers our ability to trace the development of pin types throughout the Mycenaean period. Even the evidence from the Citadel House Area must be evaluated with care, since much material of LH IIIC date represents collapsed debris and wash levels. Thus individual items may

PLATE 17

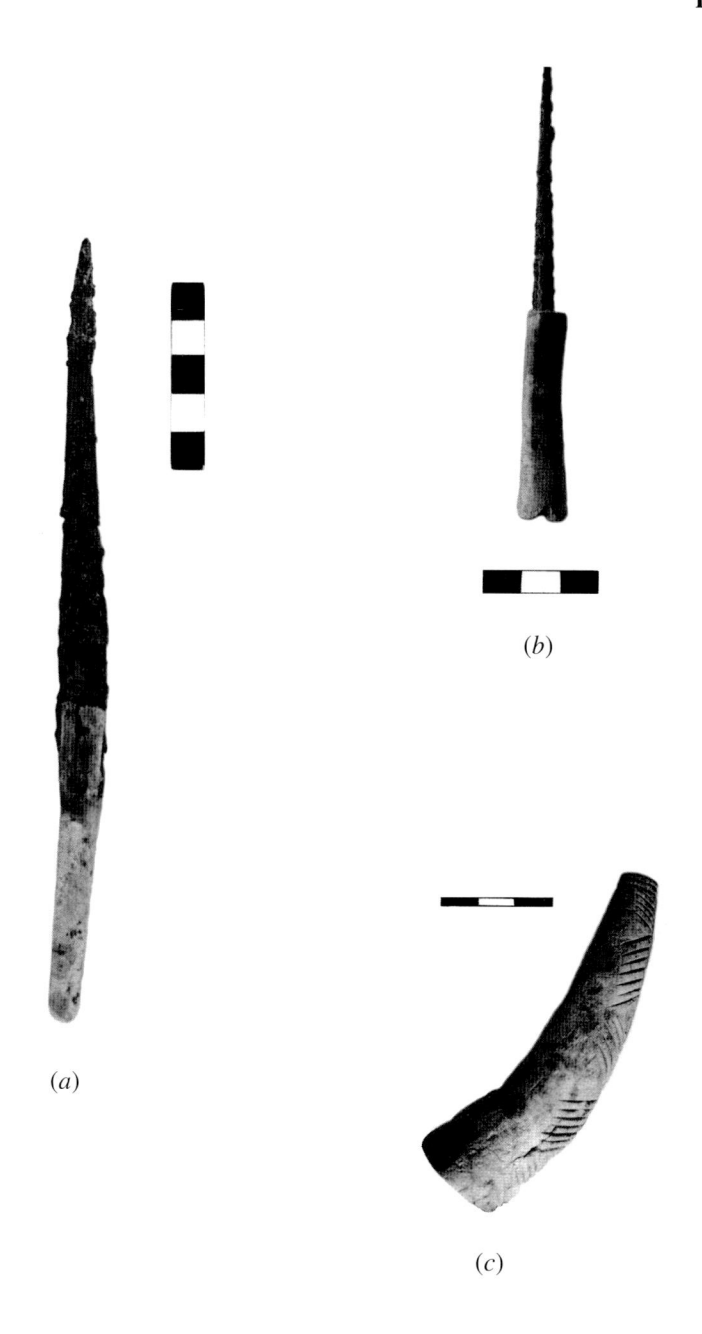

(*a*)

(*b*)

(*c*)

Handles of bone and antler: (*a*) **B/I-1**; (*b*) **B-3**; (*c*) **A-1**.

65

PLATE 18

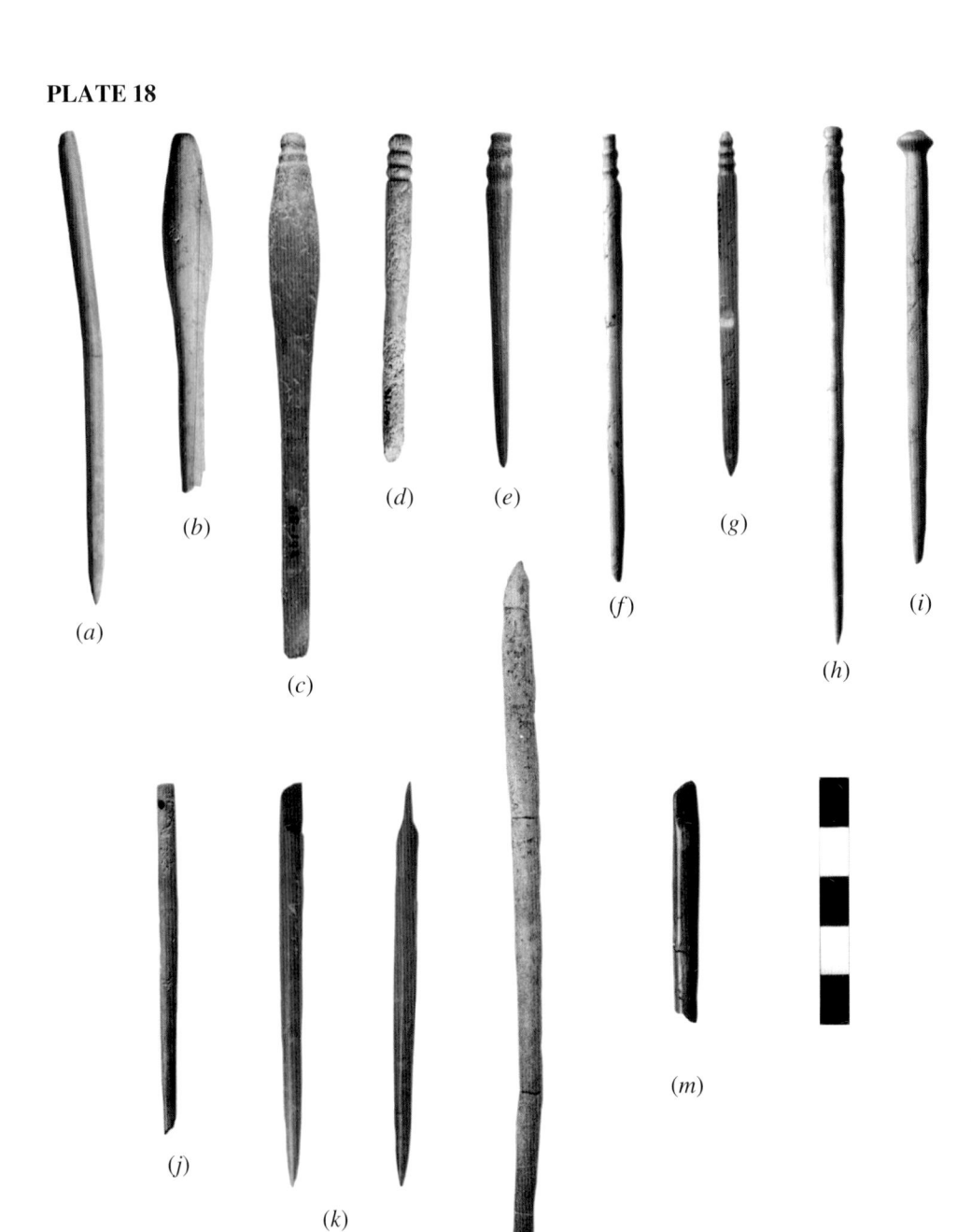

Bone pins and spatulae. Pins: (*a*) **B-4**; (*b*) **B-11**; (*c*) **B-12**; (*d*) **B-17**; (*e*) **B-18**; (*f*) **B-19**; (*g*) **B-20**; (*h*) **B-21**; (*i*) **B-22**. Needle: (*j*) **B-27**. 'Spatulae': (*k*) **B-28**; (*l*) **B-29**; (*m*) **B-30**.

not be in their primary context. None the less, in view of the difficulties outlined above, our collection of dated examples offers welcome information.

Plain pins have a long history on the Greek mainland, going back to the MH period (e.g. *Asea*, 130, fig. 121.18), if not earlier. They seem to persist until the LH IIIC period, since five examples (**B-6** to **B-10**) were recovered from phase X and XI contexts in the Citadel House Area and an unfinished example (**B-69**) was found in a phase X floor deposit (above p. 60). As far as one can tell, the type changes little if at all through time. The same also seems to be true of pins with ribbed heads, also attested on the mainland from the MH period onwards (e.g. *Asine* I, 255, fig. 180.12). The examples from the Citadel House Area were found in all of the main LBA levels (bar phase VIII). In other words, the type was in use until the end of the LH IIIC period, if not later. One wonders if it is significant that the two pins (**B-21** and **B-22**) found in or near SM/PG graves had been re-worked, following damage to their heads. A small pin with a ribbed head (**B-25**) was found in the Hellenistic levels XIV, while two more (**B-23** and **B-24**) came from mixed contexts, which included a wide range of material.

Our pins with bulbous heads are especially interesting. These were recovered in LH IIIC contexts only, although it is worth remembering that few pins of any kind came from the main phase VII and VIII levels. However, it is possible that this variety was a late addition to the repertoire. There are few clear antecedents in the LH IIIB period, whereas bronze pins with bulbous shafts do occur in sub-Mycenaean contexts, e.g. J. Deshayes, *Deiras*, pl. 100.1 (Argos T. XX) and H. Müller-Karpe, *JdI* 77 (1962) 86, figs. 3.1–2, 4.1–2, 10–11 (Kerameikos).

Fine needles of bone or ivory are surprisingly rare in the Aegean Bronze Age, although inadequate publication may be partly to blame for the scarcity of comparanda. It is also possible that some of the ubiquitous 'pin fragments' are, in reality, broken needles. Bone needles are attested at Lerna IV (e.g. Banks 1967, 423, 426–7, especially cat. no. 1115) and an ivory example was found at Mycenae in the Prehistoric Cemetery (52-538). Although our needles were found in LH IIIB levels, the type apparently persisted into the LH IIIC period (see p. 334 for references).

'Spatulae'

This category includes five objects of unknown purpose, spatulate at one end and tapering to a pin-like point at the other. The three found in LH IIIB levels (**B-28** to **B-30**, Figs. 11–12, Pl. 18) are finely worked and belong to a well-defined type, with good parallels from the acropolis at Mycenae, Tiryns and Thebes. The two from Hellenistic contexts (**B-31**, **B-32**, Fig. 14) are very different in appearance and are altogether much cruder implements. They did not necessarily have the same function. Here discussion will focus on those definitely Mycenaean.

In all about two dozen 'spatulae' have been recovered from Mycenaean sites, but few are published. Most have been examined by the present writer and permit the following observations (see p. 337 for complete list).[9] All seem to be made from bone, and not ivory or antler. Complete examples range in length from *c*. 0.06–0.15 m (e.g. **B-29**). The standards of workmanship range from good to excellent; in this respect they resemble fine pins. At one end the cylindrical shaft tapers to a very fine point, at the other the shaft is bevelled from both sides. This spatulate end is usually cut at an oblique angle; the edge is sometimes sharp and may be slightly bevelled from wear (e.g. **B-28**). In other cases the spatulate end is very worn and blunt (e.g. **B-30**). Sometimes the tip of the pointed end is worn, sometimes it is fine and quite sharp (e.g. **B-28**). Apart from these minor differences, all examples are remarkably similar. Here it should be noted that the object described as a 'stylus' and thought to be suitable for use on papyrus (*WBM* 1, 41–2) is actually an unfinished bone pin (**B-68**).

Several interpretations have been offered for these enigmatic objects. Initially the examples from the Citadel House Area were regarded as 'cosmetic implements'. The high quality of workmanship and fine polish would support this view and conceivably the spatulate end could have been used for mixing or applying cosmetics. But these arguments are hardly compelling. The discovery of an example in a 'jewellery workshop' at Thebes led the excavator, Dr Katie Demakopoulou, to suggest it could have been used for applying gold leaf (*AAA* 7 (1974) 167, fig. 5). While a better term might be 'gold foil', her idea is attractive on two counts. It is supported by context and would certainly account for the distinctive shape of both spatulate and pointed ends. Finally, Professor Louis Godart identified the examples from Tiryns as 'Linear B styli' and used two of them to write imitation tablets (*AA* 1988, 248–51). But the fact that these objects *can* be used for writing on clay does not settle the issue satisfactorily. Several crucial points remain unanswered, not least whether both ends were used for writing. Godart's account was silent on this issue and correspondence likewise failed to provide clarification (24.12.1984). Several Linear B scholars have expressed reservations as to whether the pointed ends were really sharp and fine enough (e.g. J. Chadwick, in litt. 9.4.1985). This concern was reinforced when unpublished examples from Mycenae in the National Museum were examined alongside tablets from Pylos. However, the discovery of a wooden writing board, originally covered in wax, in the Uluburun wreck (*AJA* 93 (1989) 10–11, fig. 19; *Anatolian Studies* 41 (1991) 99–106, pls. 17–18) now raises the possibility that similar boards were also used in Mycenaean Greece. The features of our 'spatulae' seem to me eminently well suited to writing on wax tablets (cf. **B-31** and **B-32** below).

Unfortunately few of these objects come from informative contexts. The four bone implements from Tiryns came from LH IIIB1 and IIIB2 contexts in the Unterburg, while the possible bronze example was found with LH IIIA1 material beneath the Small Megaron (*AA* 1988, 250–1). Essentially they appear to be stray finds; none was found with Linear B tablets. As already noted, one from Thebes came from a 'jewellery workshop'; two more came from chamber tombs (14 and 15) on the Kolonaki Hill (*AD* 3 (1917) 151, 177, fig. 129.11).[10] In addition, three or four examples were found in the Lianka plot at Thebes, which yielded 56 inscribed clay nodules (*AD* 38 (1983) Chr. 132–3; cf. *BCH* 114 (1990) 103ff). However, the room contained a wide range of finds, including stone vases, steatite conuli, bone tools, ivory plaque fragments, terracotta figurines, shells, obsidian, lead and a small Cycladic figurine. In any case, since we are not sure where the nodules were written, the necessary link to the 'spatulae' remains elusive. It is also worth observing that no objects of this type are known from Pylos or from the Houses outside the Citadel at Mycenae, which also yielded tablets and inscribed sealings.

The three examples from the Citadel House Area do not resolve the question of function. An unusually fine example (**B-28**) — almost in mint condition — was found in the phase VII deposit in Room II. This also yielded much ivory 'workshop material' (p. 6, Fig. 4) and thirteen unworked boar's tusks (below p. 77) and much else. Unfortunately there is nothing to enlighten us here. **B-30**, badly worn and lacking its pointed end, came from the phase VIII floor in Room 1, apparently a storeroom. Nearby in Room 5 a third example **B-29** came to light in calcined debris, evidently fallen from the room above during the phase VIII destruction. Similar debris in Corridor 4 yielded 7 Linear B tablets 'embedded in hard calcine or fused mud-brick'

(*WBM* 1, 27; *MT* III, 41 figs. 81–2). Although **B-29** has survived complete, it was broken and heavily burnt to a bluish-white colour. While here we seem to have another possible association between inscriptions and a 'spatula' or 'stylus', it is worth stressing that the objects are in secondary contexts, having been displaced in the great LH IIIB2 destruction. Moreover, as noted elsewhere, finds from the Citadel House Area — and references to *kuanos* workers on the tablets — suggest that jewellery working occurred somewhere in the vicinity. Thus we should remain open to the suggestion that these distinctive objects played a role in jewellery manufacture. For the matter to be resolved we clearly need more finds from less ambiguous contexts. But progress could also be made through a study of micro-wear patterns, examined under a Scanning Electron Microscope.[11]

The function of the two Hellenistic examples (**B-31** and **B-32**, Fig. 14) is also open to question. They resemble objects frequently described as 'styli' in the literature, although J. M. Stubbings, in her detailed account of the Perachora examples, admits: 'one cannot say for certain that they were not used for toilet purposes such as the spreading of ointment or even as pins' (*Perachora* II, 445ff, pl. 189). However, she also observes that the form — with a pointed end for inscribing on wax and a spatulate end for erasing — appears in representations from the sixth century BC onwards. The basic shape is remarkably long-lived, persisting down to the Hellenistic or Roman period, though on some the length of the spatulate end is exaggerated (e.g. *Corinth* XII, 185–7, pl. 183).

Fragments of pins, needles or 'spatulae'

These items have carefully worked cylindrical shafts and sometimes preserve a pointed end, but their heads are lacking (**B-33** to **B-46**). In all 14 examples were found, recovered in all levels except VI, XI and XII. Fragments like these are ubiquitous on sites of all periods.

Miscellaneous

B-47 (Fig. 12) is a plano-convex disc with a large piercing; perhaps it served as an ornament or button. It was found among destruction debris in Corridor 4. Two items might be broken pin heads or possibly toggles: **B-48** (Fig. 13) is a cylindrical segment with a series of 17 rather crude incisions around it, while **B-50** (Fig. 15) consists of two barrel-shaped elements separated by a flat torus. It is decorated with incised circles and dots. **B-48** came from the phase IX floor in Room xxi, **B-50** was associated with Hellenistic and LH IIIC material. **B-49** (Fig. 13) is a curious object, having a wedge-shaped 'blade' and a narrow neck, which is pierced transversely. Since the neck is broken it is difficult to reconstruct the original shape, much less guess the likely function. It was found with phase XI and XII material in Room 15B. Finally, a small carinated button or bead (**B-51**) came from Hellenistic levels.

Tools

The fifteen bone tools found on the site are a disappointing lot (see Figs. 10–13, 15, Pl. 19). They do not readily lend themselves to classification, though this is usually the case with small collections (see comment on ivories above, p. 3). Two short and slender examples (**B-56** and **B-63**) are made from long bones of small mammals (not identified). For another small tool (**B-52**) a heavily worked splinter of bone was used, while a fourth (**B-57**) is much more irregular. Other examples are made from more substantial segments of long bones: **B-54**, **B-60**, **B-62**, **B-64** and **B-66**. Even among these much variation can be observed in size (L. *c.* 0.04–0.09 m), shape and working ends (blunt or sharp). Casual points like these can occur on almost any ancient site, but rarely will one find an exact match. Two pierced tools are much more distinctive. One (**B-55**) has a rather flat head, which retains some of the natural concavity of the bone, although the shaft has been worked to a cylindrical section; the 'eye' is fairly small (D. 0.003 m). The second (**B-59**) is made from a broad segment of bone, rectangular in section at the butt end, but becoming rounder toward the short and stubby point. Here the 'eye' measures D. 0.004 m. It is, however, doubtful whether either tool served as a needle, i.e. the piercing may have been for suspension. Similar objects, known from the EBA onwards, shed no light on the issue. Two or three tools were made from split rib bones: **B-58**, **B-65** and perhaps also the tiny fragment **B-61**. **B-58** is leaf-shaped, well worn and rounded at the butt end, while the pointed end is sharp and rather jagged. Here there is little sign of wear and one wonders if the point had been damaged and re-cut. Finally, a cattle rib (not split) was used for **B-53**: along one edge are 24 short sturdy teeth, now very smooth from use. Coarse combs of this type are not common, though they are attested on the mainland at Lerna (periods IV–V) as well as Eleusis and Krisa in the MH period (see p. 364 for references). To my knowledge only one coarse comb comes from a secure LH context: an example from Lerna VII made of antler main beam (Wiencke 1998, 175 fig. 29, pl. 30).

Most if not all of the bone tools from the Citadel House Area seem to be strays. This is in marked contrast to the antler tools, which are concentrated in phase VII deposits in Room 32 and Area 36 (p. 56 and below pp. 74–6). Four bone tools were found below the main phase VII floors (**B-52** to **B-55**). **B-56** was found on the floor in Room 31, while **B-58** was associated with the backfill in Room 32. **B-57** came from the phase VII floor deposit in Area 36, but cannot certainly be linked to activities there. Four more tools were found with material dating to the phase VIII destruction: **B-59** from Room 18; **B-60** to **B-62** in Passage 34. Three more (**B-63** to **B-65**) come from phase X; another (**B-66**) was found with mixed LBA to Hellenistic material. This scattered distribution makes it well nigh impossible to draw useful conclusions about our small collection. It should, at least, help to abolish the myth that bone tools had no place in LBA palatial centres. In fact many examples, never published, were found by Schliemann and Tsountas on the acropolis. Sadly, without a provenance, they offer scant clues as to why, how and when they were used.

Partly worked bone
Among the 10 items in this category are both unfinished objects and cut segments, which are probably waste from earlier processes. The three unfinished objects are by far the most interesting. The first (**B-67**, Fig. 12, Pl. 19) is particularly odd. It is a cylindrical object (L. 0.97, D. max. 0.021 m) made from solid bone, pierced transversely near one end. It resembles no known object. More perplexing still is the source of the bone: no domesticated animal has bones that would yield a diameter of 0.021 m. A wild ox (*Bos primigenius*) is a possibility, though this remains little more than an educated guess, since all diagnostic features of the bone were removed in working.[12] The irregular tool marks and a rough protrusion from sawing at one end suggest that the object was unfinished. Elsewhere tool marks may have been smoothed away, though the surface is not polished. Unfortunately the context — the phase VIII floor in Passage 34 — is uninformative.

With our next two objects (**B-68** and **B-69**, Fig. 13, Pl. 19) we are on safer ground. These are certainly unfinished pins, which have reached a fairly advanced stage in manufacture. **B-**

PLATE 19

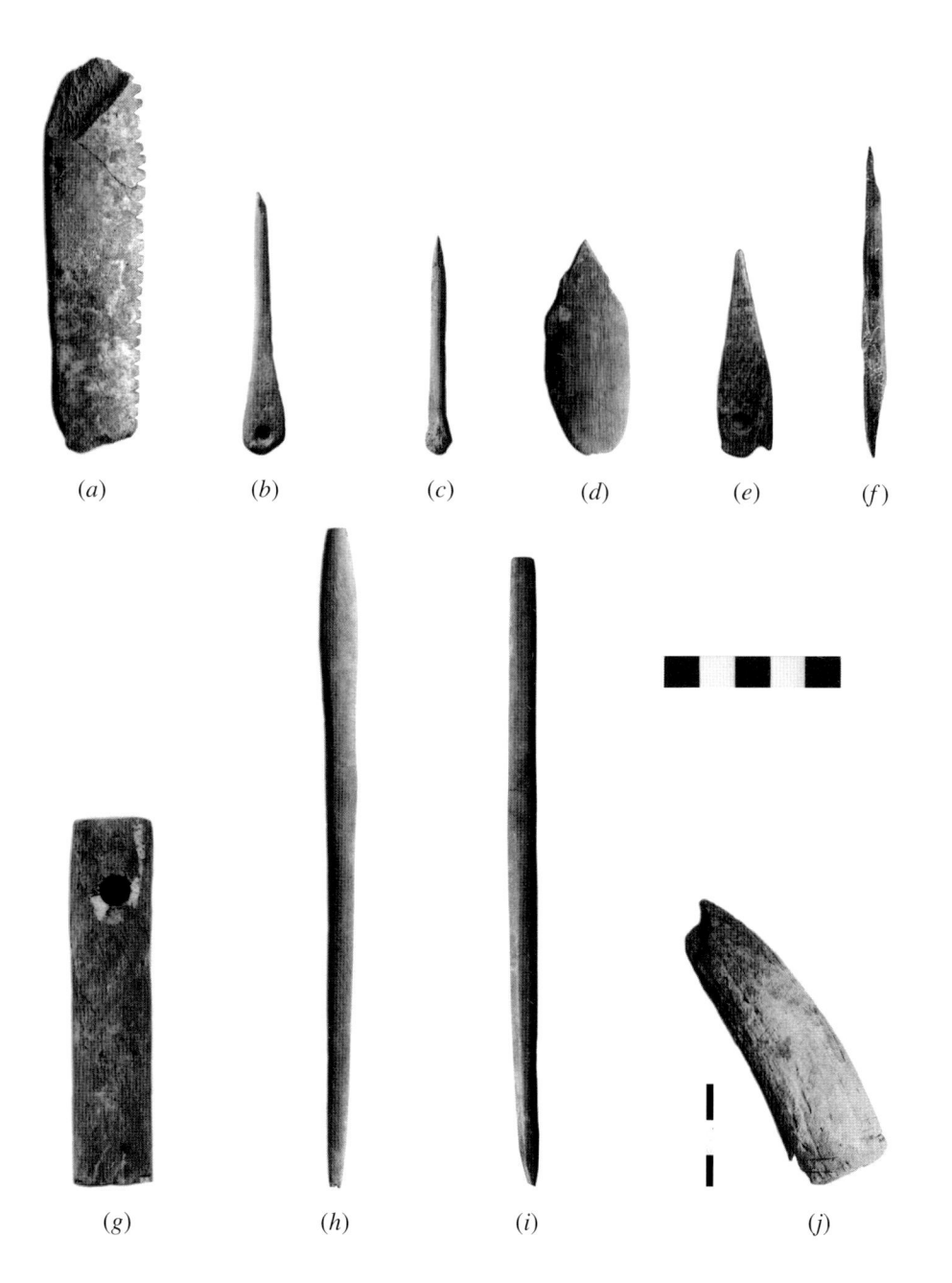

Bone tools: (*a*) **B-53**; (*b*) **B-55**; (*c*) **B-56**; (*d*) **B-58**; (*e*) **B-59**; (*f*) **B-64**; (*g*) **B-67**; (*h*) **B-68**; (*i*) **B-69**. Horn core: (*j*) **H-1**.

69 has a long straight shaft, roughly hexagonal in section, tapering slightly to the pointed end. Tool marks are visible along all the facets. The shape would have been produced by working down a blank — wedge-shaped in section — cut from a cattle (or deer) metapodial. **B-69** needed little more work to produce a finished pin with a plain head. Rubbing with coarse abrasives, e.g. a sandstone block, would smooth the facets into a cylindrical shaft. Finer abrasives would be used in polishing. **B-68** is a very similar object, of comparable dimensions, abandoned at much the same stage in manufacture. It is certainly not a 'stylus' as originally thought (see above pp. 67–8; *WBM* 1, 40–1). Rather, a bulbous-headed pin was the intended end-product, with the upper end of the shaft swelling slightly before tapering toward the head. Unfortunately **B-68** was found with collapsed phase IX debris in Room xxi and was not *in situ*. However the LH IIIC date would accord with the distribution of other bulbous-headed pins on the site (see above p. 67). **B-69** was found on the phase X floor in Room liii. The same context yielded a very irregular splinter of bone (**B-71**). Although at first sight this might seem to be another unfinished pin, it was probably waste from other processes.

Several partly worked segments have been carefully cut from long bones. These include two similar pieces (**B-72** and **B-73**, Fig. 13) found with collapsed phase X debris over Room xxx. Although segments of this shape might serve as blanks, e.g. for inlay manufacture, it is more likely that we are dealing with waste. In other words, the neatly cut ends result from removing the epiphyses (joints), a preliminary step before extracting wedge-shaped segments for pins (see above). **B-70** (Fig. 13) is also likely to be waste from making pins or tools; it is too small to be of much value as a blank. This was found below the phase X floor overlying Room 31 and may be a stray from LH IIIB. A very long segment (**B-74**, Fig. 14), neatly cut, was found beneath the floor of Hellenistic Yard HH. A small piece of scrap (**B-75**, Fig. 15) was recovered from cleaning.

HORN CORE

As already noted, horns — carried by sheep/goat, cattle and antelope — consist of an inner bony core and an outer keratinous sheath, i.e. the material 'horn'. This material does not survive archaeologically in the Aegean, although the bony cores do. Occasionally these make their way into small find lots, as **H-1** has done. Here we are dealing with the horn core of a goat, probably male, which had been hacked off at the proximal end (Fig. 11, Pl. 19). This is the normal means of removing horns from the frontal bone of the skull. Deep incisions (perhaps trial cuts) occur roughly parallel to the cut end. Unfortunately it is impossible to be certain that the keratinous sheath was still on the core at the time of destruction. If so, then the horn may have been stored pending manufacture. Had the sheath already been removed for use, then the core was simply waste. The context — Room 32 — can provide no answers, since among the partly worked ivories found there were waste segments (e.g. **I-75**) as well as the large cube (**I-70**).

The extent to which horn was exploited in the LBA Aegean cannot be gauged. There are few systematic studies of faunal material and, as already noted, horn cores are only rarely registered as small finds. One of the horn cores from Ayia Irini may have had its keratinous sheath removed (Krzyszkowska 1990, pl. 31 below). Certainly horn is a very versatile material, tough and pliable. In Egypt (where it does survive) it was used for a range of everyday utensils, including handles and vessels (Krzyszkowska and Morkot 2000, 327–38; also Hodges 1964, 153ff).

ANTLER

Antlers are bony outgrowths from skulls of male deer, which develop annually and then are shed following the rutting season (Krzyszkowska 1990, 58–64). Thus antler may be acquired from freshly killed carcasses or collected after the rut. Although shed antler is said to be harder to work than fresh, evidence from Ayia Irini indicates that both forms were used on Kea during the Bronze Age (Krzyszkowska 1990, 64, pl. 26). The use of antler in the Aegean, however, is not well documented. Indeed in the published literature it has fared even worse than bone and misidentification is a major problem (above p. 54). This is a shame, because antler was certainly available throughout the Greek mainland and provides a versatile alternative to bone. Indeed its most important property — resilience under pressure — made it more suitable than bone for tools subjected to repeated stress. For this reason antler was often used in antiquity for picks, e.g. in flint-mining. Virtually all of the worked antler known from the Aegean comes from red deer, although fallow deer — with their distinctive palmate antlers — appear in pictorial representations (e.g. West House frieze: Doumas 1992, pl. 71; Tiryns fresco: Immerwahr 1990, 130–2, fig. 36). Roe deer also probably existed on the mainland, although their antlers are very small. By contrast, mature red deer carry antlers of considerable size and the main beam is long and straight (Krzyszkowska 1990, 60, figs. 24, 26). Thus pointed tools like those found in the Citadel House Area (**A-3** to **A-15**) are often made from segments of main beam. The tines or prongs were also used, usually for tools and handles (e.g. **A-1**). Small decorative objects, including pins and inlays, could also be fashioned from antler. Of course, when heavily worked and polished the material could easily be mistaken for bone (or even ivory). Thus, an effective substitute in antiquity can all too easily confuse the modern archaeologist (e.g. **A/B-2**; cf. Krzyszkowska 1990, pls. 29–30).

The Citadel House Area has yielded a small but exceptionally interesting collection of antler objects (**A-1** to **A-15**) and two pieces of partly worked antler (**A-16** to **A-17**). The **handle** (**A-1**, Fig. 13, Pl. 17) was made from a whole tine with its tip removed (cf. Krzyszkowska 1990, pls. 28–9). At this end the natural spongy interior of the antler was slightly hollowed out to take a bronze tool. Now only tiny traces of bronze remain *in situ*, but the tool was probably a slender awl similar to that preserved in **B-3**. Around the small end are two neat grooves, while a chevron design is incised along the outer curve. Antler tines fit comfortably in the hand and the spongy interior helps to absorb shock. Yet for all their suitability, published comparanda are all but non-existent. The 'horn' handle with incised decoration reported from Eutresis must be made from an antler tine (Goldman, *Eutresis*, 215, fig. 284.20). Undecorated handles which have lost their bronze tools might easily be overlooked. There is an unpublished example from Lerna VI, while another from Ayia Irini seems to be unfinished (*Keos* III, 54, cat. no. 137). The antler handle from Tiryns in which a bronze chisel is preserved seems to be made from main beam (*Tiryns* V, 15, pl. 23.2–4).

Pin

A short pin with a ribbed head (**A/B-2**, Fig. 13) may be made from antler, although there is some room for doubt. The material closely resembles the smooth working ends of the antler tools (e.g. **A-6**). The rounded tip and ribbed head with its 'soft' profile are also consistent with antler, a material which is less dense than bone. Although antler is rarely used for pins and needles, examples have been identified at Ayia Irini (e.g. *Keos* VII, 70, pl. 116 BG-39 pin, period IV;

Krzyszkowska 1990, pl. 30b needle, LH IIIA). Elsewhere antler pins might have passed unnoticed. Our example was found with collapsed phase X debris over Room xxx.

Tools

The discovery of antler tools on the site is both important and intriguing. Eight of the thirteen examples were associated with phase VII deposits in the Room with the Fresco Complex and the adjacent Area 36 (Fig. 11, Pl. 20). The tools are remarkably homogeneous in appearance, though few are now complete and many are friable. Most if not all seem to be flat segments of main beam: the longest examples reach L. 0.18–0.20 m (e.g. **A-3**, **A-7** and **A-8**). There is very little variation in width (W.0.014–0.019 m). The tools are carefully fashioned with long regular lateral edges, but only at the working end proper are the natural features of the antler wholly obliterated. Thus traces of the ridged outer cortex usually exist on the upper surfaces, while cancellous material, slightly smoothed, occurs on the undersides. Patches where these features are worn away offer clues as to how the tools were held. For instance, a clear thumb-rest occurs mid-way along the shaft of **A-8** on the upper surface; corresponding patches on the underside were probably worn smooth by the fingers. Lateral edges are generally smooth, sometimes very smooth, either caused by handling or possibly by use. The working ends rarely exceed L. 0.03 m, which prompts us to wonder why the tools were so long. There is some variation in the shape of the working ends. A few taper evenly to a fine tip, round or ovoid in section (e.g. **A-4** and **A-6**). Others have an asymmetrical working end and a flattened tip (e.g. **A-8**). These variations could reflect the working habits of different individuals. However, we cannot be certain that all examples were used for the same task. Indeed, it is even possible for one tool to be used in a variety of ways, making it well nigh impossible to decipher accurately the patterns of wear.

The purpose of the tools, then, remains enigmatic. There is little doubt that the choice of antler was deliberate — perhaps for its resilience under pressure, perhaps for the straight lengths offered by main beams. But the length of the tools remains one of their most puzzling features, since the working ends are relatively short and only the very tips (rarely more than L. 0.01 m) were heavily used. While one or two are probably fine enough for piercing, we cannot be certain that this was how they were employed. In other cases the wear pattern seems to be caused by short backward and forward movements, perhaps associated with rubbing or smoothing. It has already been suggested that these tools (or some of them) played a role in glass and gold working, which may have occurred somewhere in the vicinity of the site. Indeed, U-shaped 'whorls' exist on several glass relief ornaments, which correspond quite well to the wear patterns seen on some of our tools.[13] Systematic study of tool marks on glass objects, supported by experimental replication and SEM studies (see n. 11) could offer a way forward, but in practice these would be extremely hard to organize. For the foreseeable future we will have to content ourselves with more rigorous macroscopic examination of jewellery and better documentation of antler tools.

Trawling through the existing literature for comparanda proves a thankless task. Happily, unpublished examples are known from Ayia Irini, Lefkandi, Lerna, Tiryns and even from the acropolis at Mycenae.[14] And it is very likely that others lurk unidentified in site or museum apothekes. For instance, an important series of antler tools found during the Swedish excavations at Malthi (Valmin 1938) has only recently been published (Blitzer 1991, 37–9, cat. nos. 161–73).[15] Among the pointed tools are several possible parallels (cat. nos. 161–4) for the Mycenae examples. But superficial similarities may mask quite different functions: Blitzer has suggested that the Malthi tools may have been used for pressure-flaking in the chipped stone industry. Nor

PLATE 20

(a)   (b)   (c)   (d)   (e)

Antler tools: (*a*) **A-3**; (*b*) **A-6**; (*c*) **A-7**; (*d*) **A-8**; (*e*) **A-10**.

are the Malthi examples securely dated, although Blitzer states that they occurred in MH–LH deposits. Evidence from other sites suggests that pointed tools (similar to ours) may be a LBA phenomenon. At Lerna, for instance, antler tools made from whole tines exist in periods III, IV and V (Banks 1967, 466–71). But the only pointed tools made from heavily worked segments of main beam were found in period VI.[16] A similar pattern may be observed at Ayia Irini, which has significant amounts of worked, partly worked and unworked antler from period IV (MBA onwards). Only in the LBA levels do we find pointed tools made from segments of main beam (e.g. Krzyszkowska 1990, pl. 30a).

Major LBA palatial centres have also yielded antler tools. Those from Mycenae found by Schliemann and Tsountas languish in the Athens National Museum and have no known provenance, but there is better hope for those discovered at Tiryns.[17] Thebes probably offers the best chance of finding more examples in informative contexts. One, discovered in the 'jewellery workshop' on the Kouropoulos plot, has already been published (*AAA* 7 (1974) 167, 173, fig. 5).[18] And our collection should now help focus attention on this intriguing tool type. The pattern of distribution in the Citadel House Area is certainly striking: two in Room 32 (**A-3** and **A-4**), another in Room 31 (**A-5**, surely a stray) and five more from Area 36 (**A-6** to **A-10**). This concentration is in marked contrast to the scatter of bone tools, found throughout most levels (see above). Only two antler tools were associated with phase IX material (**A-11** found during cleaning of walls ac/ab (Room xxi); and **A-12** in Room xxxiii). Although they differ in shape, it is possible that they are earlier products displaced and re-deposited following the LH IIIB destructions. One wonders if the same is true for **A-13** from the Hellenistic Yard HH and two fragmentary examples (**A-14** and **A-15**) found during cleaning.

Partly worked antler

Two small pieces of partly worked antler — both segments of tines — contribute nothing to our understanding of the antler tools. Both pieces are certainly strays: **A-16** (Fig. 10) was found in the construction levels beneath Room 15, while **A-17** (Fig. 11) came from the Alcove of Room 18. A large piece of ?red deer antler was found among very disturbed material in Gamma 10 (Γ10'62/76 MM 22115, Rm xlii, Phase 0849/1111/1149), though its heavily burnt and calcined condition probably indicate a phase VIII origin. [It was not catalogued and is a shed piece showing no sign of working per Dr Umberto Albarella.]

BOAR'S TUSK

In the LBA Aegean boar's tusk was chiefly used for making plates to cover helmets. The plates ordinarily have small holes for attachment to a leather cap, and were disposed in overlapping rows. Finds of helmet plates and pictorial representations suggest that this helmet type was particularly widespread in LB I–II occurring not only on the Greek mainland, but also on Crete and the Cycladic islands (Barbarigos 1991).

The tusks used for helmet plates are curving lower canines, which are trihedral in section (Krzyszkowska 1990, 47–9, fig. 20, pls. 18–19). Two faces of the tusks are covered with hard glistening enamel, which offers several benefits to the owner of a helmet. Not only is the material itself attractive, the enamel registers about 7 on the Mohs scale, i.e. roughly equivalent to semi-precious stones. Thus plates would provide an effective protection against offensive weapons.

A boar's tusk helmet surely also conferred prestige, since about 40 tusks might be required to make one. Plates were made by sectioning a tusk lengthwise and discarding the face that lacks enamel. Usually remains of the pulp cavity occur on the underside of plates. Tusks of mature animals would obviously be favoured, since these would yield larger plates. However, we have few data on 'average' sizes of boar's tusks for the Aegean.

Helmet plates
In the Citadel House Area only 4 helmet plates came to light (Pl. 21). Two were recovered in early contexts, pre-dating the main phase VII construction (**BT-1** and **BT-2**, Fig. 10). They could easily be strays from graves in the cemetery area. The same could also apply to a large plate from Room II (**BT-3**). Another plate was found with material of mixed LBA and Hellenistic date (**BT-4**, Fig. 15).

Unworked boar's tusks
Thirteen unworked tusks (**BT-8** to **BT-14**, Pl. 21) were found in Room II (phase VII). As already noted, this room also contained numerous inlays and partly worked ivory (p. 6). The concentration of tusks here suggests that they had been deliberately collected and were being stored for eventual use. That said, there is some doubt as to whether boar's tusk helmets were still made in the Late Mycenaean period. Our scattered helmet plates shed no light on the issue, while plates in late graves could well be heirlooms (as in Homer, *Iliad* X. 261 ff). It may be that by LH IIIB the boar's tusk helmet had been largely replaced by new and more efficient types. A possible decline in populations (e.g. caused by land clearance and hunting) may also have been a factor. Nevertheless the tusks found in Room II should prompt us to keep an open mind. Some of them (e.g. **BT-13**) were sizeable and could certainly have been used for making plates. By contrast, a few other scattered tusks on the site seem to be nothing more than discards from consumption of boar or pig meat (e.g. **BT-7**, **BT-15**).

PLATE 21

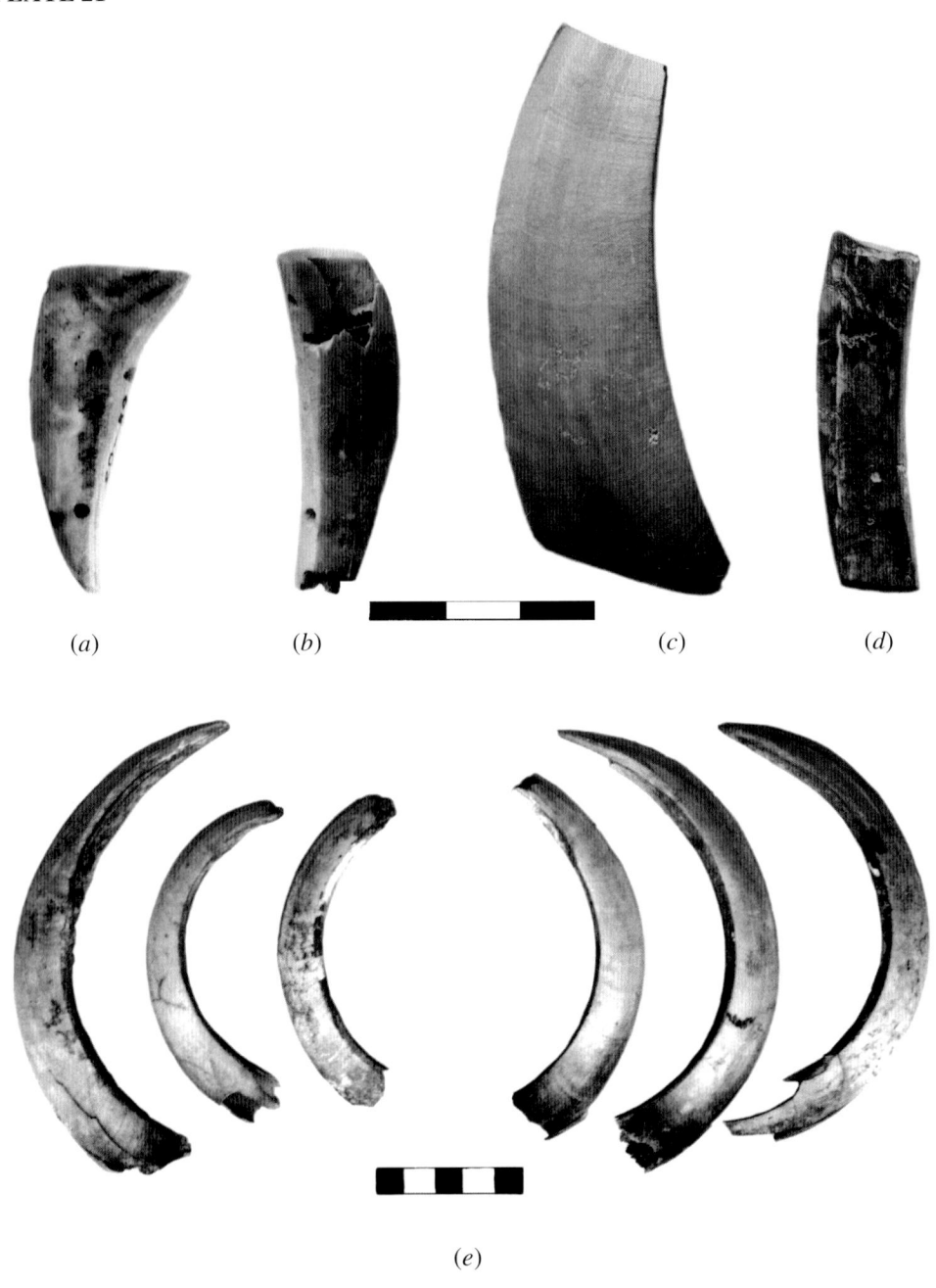

(a) (b) (c) (d)

(e)

Boar's tusks: (a) **BT-1**; (b) **BT-2**; (c) **BT-3**; (d) **BT-4**; (e) Room II group including **BT-9**, **BT-10**, **BT-12** and **BT-14**. (a–d) Scale 1:1.

ENDNOTES

1. He worked on the acropolis in 1886, 1888, 1890, 1892, 1893, 1895 and 1896, with reconstruction work on the acropolis and elsewhere in 1897. Some of ivories are included in Poursat 1977*b* nos. 20–48, many more languish in the National Museum Athens (see n. 5). For the Schliemann ivories see below n. 4 and Poursat 1977*b* nos. 1–19.
2. The hilt-plates were first identified as such by Mrs Diana Wardle in her study of the bronzes from the site in 1980 (see Wardle and Wardle 1997, 68, 114).
3. In some copies of Krzyszkowska 1992*a*, cube **I-70** illustrated on pl. 1b, was incorrectly orientated (by the printer). This was corrected in the 2nd impression.
4. They may have been grouped together by the museum as miscellaneous pieces, although the range of material is comparable to that found in Room II and Room 32. The 10 pieces illustrated by Poursat (1977*b*, cat. no. 19, pl. III) include: 8 segments of partly worked ivory (some orientated incorrectly), one damaged acorn-shaped object (cf. **I-24**) and a fragmentary relief (?) plaque. It is not possible to determine if the last two items were finished objects or if they were mistakes / rejects / salvage. In addition NM 1022 includes: 4 fragments of inlay strips, several fragments of dog-tooth inlays, a fragmentary knife handle (similar to **I-22**) and 4 small pieces of waste ivory. It is also uncertain whether the many pins, needles and tools (of bone and antler) from Schliemann's excavations, collected under NM 1060, were found together.
5. I am deeply grateful to Dr Katie Demakopoulou for allowing me to see this material, which was apparently first inventoried in the early 1970s.
6. The material is currently under study for a Heidelberg dissertation by Miss Athina Papadakis. I am most grateful to the excavator Dr Vassilis Aravantinos and to Miss Papadakis for showing me this material in September 2001, as well as the ivories and hippopotamus lower canine published in Aravantinos 2000.
7. The glass seal (68-1545: *CMS* V no. 598) cannot be 'unfinished' as reported in *WBM* 10, 111 (apparently misunderstanding a pers. comm. from Hughes-Brock to French). No amount of additional work would change its unusual appearance: kidney-shaped with a flat back (examined 9/01). Ordinarily pressed glass seals (i.e. made in moulds) are lentoids with conical backs. A few other flat-backed examples do exist, including four seals from the same mould: *CMS* V Suppl. 1B nos. 132, 133, 451 and *CMS* VII no. 137. The kidney-shape is unique and results from a mishap during manufacture (cf. Tamvaki 1974, 262 n. 27). I cordially thank Professor Ingo Pini for discussing this piece with me. Only a handful of pressed glass seals are known from the Argolid, whereas more than 70 have been found in 'peripheral' areas: see now Dickers 2001, 77–86.
8. The study of the faunal material from the CHA by Dr Umberto Albarella is in progress.
9. A more detailed account, in preparation, will include the unpublished examples from Mycenae (excavated by Schliemann and Tsountas).
10. Apart from the 'stylus' T.19 contained many rich finds; Kilian's idea that the deceased may have been a 'palace scribe' is surely fanciful (*AA* 1988, 251). No objects of this type are preserved from the Mycenae chamber tombs.
11. Every material (e.g. clay, leather, cloth) leaves a distinctive wear pattern on the tool used to work it. Furthermore patterns are specific to activity (e.g. piercing, rubbing etc.). A Scanning Electron Microscope (SEM) can isolate these distinctive micro-wear traces provided the tools have not been vigorously cleaned (e.g. to remove calcine encrustation). Modern copies, subjected to a range of materials and activities, must be used as controls. It goes without saying that ancient tools must never be used experimentally, since this will obliterate the original wear patterns.
12. I am grateful to Sebastian Payne for examining this piece and offering suggestions.
13. I am extremely grateful to Mrs Helen Hughes-Brock for sending me her original notes and sketches, on which she had noted traces of a U-shaped spatula(?). She had observed these on 68-1546, 68-1648 and perhaps 68-1566; also 68-1645 and perhaps 68-1556. She also commented (in litt. 16.10.85) that some 'beehive' or trochus-shell ornaments (e.g. 69-1224) show marks of a differently shaped tool with a squarer end. In addition she remarked that a pointed tool could perhaps be used for drawing out threads of contrasting colour as on the beehives. Further details will appear in H. Hughes-Brock, *WBM* 25 (in

preparation). In 1986 I was able to examine a few of the glass ornaments alongside **A-8**. The shape, size and wear patterns on the tip corresponded closely to the 'whorls' on 68-1546 and 68-1545; 68-1645 provided another possible match.

[14] I am grateful to the late Professor J. L. Caskey and the present director of the Keos project, Professor Elizabeth Schofield, for permission to publish the objects of bone, antler and ivory from Ayia Irini (in preparation). For Lerna, see below n. 16. The late Mr Mervyn Popham kindly allowed me to study drawings and records of bone and antler from Lefkandi-Xeropolis as it proved impossible to examine the objects. For Mycenae and Tiryns see below n. 17.

[15] Blitzer describes them as 'horn core', but this is an Americanism (see above p. 54). Several more antler tools (similarly described as 'horn core') were found at Nichoria. These are very short and stubby and do not appear to be good comparisons for our examples. Blitzer suggests that when hafted they could have been satisfactory punches or pressure-flaking implements: H. Blitzer, in W. A. McDonald and N. C. Wilkie (eds.), *Excavations at Nichoria in Southwest Greece* III (Minneapolis 1992) 729–30 cat. nos. 3361–5. Four come from LH deposits, two from mixed contexts.

[16] There are 5 antler tools of this variety in period VI, out of a total of 27 objects of bone, antler and boar's tusk. An account of these objects was prepared at the invitation of the late Professor J. L. Caskey in 1980 for use in his study of the Lerna Shaft Graves, but this was never published. As Caskey observed 'it is quite possible that some of these pieces are of earlier date and that they got into the graves when the pits and shafts were dug; a few even from the scarps of trenches while we were excavating' (in litt. 27.3.80). In fact few of the bone/antler finds struck me as 'earlier' in appearance. The Lerna tools are shorter than most of ours (L. avg. 0.10 m) and, of course, their function remains uncertain.

[17] The Mycenae examples were inspected, but not systematically studied, in 1986; I cordially thank Dr Katie Demakopoulou for facilitating this work. The Tiryns finds were seen in the same year, but objects of bone and antler do not appear in my study of the Tiryns ivories (Krzyszkowska 2003). Instead they will be published with other small finds from Tiryns by Dr Lorenz Rahmstorf.

[18] It is described as 'bone' and its tip has been cut off in the photograph. I was able to examine it in 1986 (thanks to the kindness of Dr Katie Demakopoulou) and can confirm that it closely resembles the Mycenae examples. As already noted, the same context yielded a 'spatula'.

BIBLIOGRAPHY AND SPECIAL ABBREVIATIONS

These include only those items which are new to this fascicule. References and abbreviations published in the introductory fascicule (*WBM* 1, 55–6) can be found on pp. 492–8. A consolidated bibliography for all fascicules will be published when the series is complete.

SPECIAL ABBREVIATIONS

IvTir (cat. no.) O. H. Krzyszkowska, 'Mycenaean ivories from Tiryns', *Tiryns* XIII (Mainz, 2005) 179–213.

BIBLIOGRAPHY

Aravantinos, V.	2000	'Nea mykenaika elephantourgemata apo ten Kadmeia (Theba)', in *Γ´ Diethnes Synedrio Boiotikon Meleton (Theba, 4–8 Septembriou 1996)* Epeteris tis Etaireias Boiotikon Meleton (Athens 2000).
Banks, E.	1967	*The Early and Middle Helladic Small Objects from Lerna* (PhD dissertation, University of Cincinnati).
Barbarigos, A. P.	1981	*To odontophrakton mykenaikon kranos* (PhD thesis, University of Athens).
Barnett, R. D.	1982	*Ancient Ivories in the Middle East.* Qedem 14 (Jerusalem).
Bass, G. F.	1987	'Oldest known shipwreck reveals Bronze Age Splendors', *National Geographic Magazine* 172.6, 693–732.
Blitzer, H.	1991	'Middle to Late Helladic chipped stone implements of the Southwest Peloponnese, Greece. Part I: the evidence from Malthi', *Hydra*, 9: *Working Papers in Middle Bronze Age Studies*, 1–71.
Catling, H. W.	1964	*Cypriot Bronzework in the Mycenaean World* (Oxford).
Caubet, A. and Poplin, F.	1987	'Les objets de matière dure animale: l'étude du matériau', in M. Yon (ed.), *Ras Shamra-Ougarit* III (Paris) 273–306.
	1992	'La place des ivoires d'Ougarit dans la production du proche orient ancient', in J. L. Fitton (ed.), *Ivory in Greece and the Eastern Mediterranean from the Bronze Age to the Hellenistic Period.* BMP Occasional Paper 85 (London) 91–100.
Cline, E. H.	1995	'Egyptian and Near Eastern imports at Late Bronze Age Mycenae', in W. V. Davies and L. Schofield (eds.), *Egypt, the Aegean and the Levant: Interconnections in the Second Millennium BC* (London) 91–115.
Demakopoulou, K. (ed.)	1988	*The Mycenaean World: Five Centuries of Early Greek Culture 1600–1100 BC* (Athens).

Demakopoulou, K. and Krzyszkowska O. H.	in prep.	'A "new" hippopotamus tusk from Mycenae'.
Demakopoulou, K., Divari-Valakou, N., Åström, P. and Walberg, G.	2000–1	'Work in Midea 1997–1999: excavation, conservation, restoration', *OpAth* 25–26, 35–52.
Dickers, A.	2001	*Die spätmykenischen Siegel aus weichem Stein*. Verlag Marie Leidorf GmbD (Rahden / Westf.).
Doumas, C.	1992	*The Wall-Paintings of Thera* (Athens).
Evans, A. J.	1930	*The Palace of Minos at Knossos* III (London).
Frankfort, H.	1970	*The Art and Architecture of the Ancient Orient* (Harmondsworth).
French, E. B.	1999	'The Room with the Fresco at the Cult Centre, Mycenae', in Y. Tzedakis and H. Martlew (eds.), *Minoans and Mycenaeans: Flavours of their Time* (Athens) 191, 194.
Goldman, H.	1931	*Excavations at Eutresis* (Cambridge, Mass.).
Hodges, H.	1964	*Artifacts: An Introduction to Early Materials and Technology* (London).
Hood, S.	1978	*The Arts in Prehistoric Greece* (Harmondsworth).
Immerwahr, S.	1990	*Aegean Painting in the Bronze Age* (University Park and London).
Krzyszkowska, O. H.	1981	'The bone and ivory industries of the Aegean Bronze Age: a technological study' (unpublished PhD thesis, University of Bristol).
	1984	'Ivory from hippopotamus tusk in the Aegean Bronze Age', *Antiquity* 58, 123–5.
	1988	'Ivory in the Aegean Bronze Age: elephant ivory or hippopotamus tusk?', *BSA* 83, 209–34.
	1990	*Ivory and Related Materials: An Illustrated Guide*. BICS Supplement 59 (London).
	1991	'The Enkomi warrior head reconsidered', *BSA* 86, 107–20.
	1992*a*	'Aegean ivory carving: towards an evaluation of LBA workshop material', in J. L. Fitton (ed.), *Ivory in Greece and the Eastern Mediterranean from the Bronze Age to the Hellenistic Period*. BMP Occasional Paper 85 (London) 25–35.
	1992*b*	'A "new" mirror handle from Cyprus', *BSA* 87, 237–42.
	1996	'Furniture in the Aegean Bronze Age', in G. Herrmann (ed.), *The Furniture of Western Asia: Ancient and Traditional* (Mainz) 85–103.
	1997	'Cult and craft: ivories from the Citadel House Area, Mycenae', in P. P. Betancourt and R. Laffineur (eds.), *TEXNH: Craftsmen, Craftswomen and Craftsmanship in the Aegean Bronze Age*. Aegaeum 16 (Liège) 145–9.

	1999	'Ivories from the Cult Centre at Mycenae', in Y. Tzedakis and H. Martlew (eds.), *Minoans and Mycenaeans: Flavours of their Time* (Athens) 195, cat. nos. 203–5.
	2005	'Mycenaean ivories from Tiryns', *Tiryns* XIII (Mainz) 179–213.
Krzyszkowska, O. H. and Morkot, R.	2000	'Ivory and related materials', in P. T. Nicholson and I. Shaw (eds.), *Ancient Egyptian Materials and Technology* (Cambridge) 320–31.
MacGillivray, J. A. et al.	2000	*The Palaikastro Kouros*. BSA Studies 6 (London).
Mylonas, G. E.	1966	'The East Wing of the Palace at Mycenae', *Hesperia* 35, 417–26.
Nicholls, R. V.	1970	'Greek votive statuettes and religious continuity, c. 1200–700 B.C.', in B. F. Harris (ed.), *Auckland Classical Essays, presented to E. M. Blaiklock* (Auckland and Oxford) 1–37.
Piteros, Chr., Olivier, J.-P. and Melena, J.	1990	'Les inscriptions en linéaire B de Thèbes (1982): la fouille, les documents, les possibilités d'interprétation', *BCH* 114, 103–84.
Poursat, J.-C.	1977*a*	*Les ivoires mycéniens* (Paris).
	1977*b*	*Catalogue des ivoires mycéniens du Musée National d'Athènes* (Paris).
Renfrew, C.	1985	*The Archaeology of Cult*. BSA Suppl. vol. 18 (London).
Safadi, H. B.	1963	'Zur Identifizierung des Elfenbeinkopfes aus Ras Shamra', *Les Annales Archéologiques de Syrie* 13, 97–106.
Sakellarakis, I.	1979	*To elephantodonto kai i katergasia tou sta mykenaïka chronia*. Bibliotheke tes en Athenais Archailogikes Etaireias 93 (Athens).
Seeden, H.	1982	'Peace figurines from the Levant', in *Archéologie au Levant: Recueil à la mémoire de Roger Saidah*. Collection de la Maison de l'Orient Méditerranéen No. 12 (Lyon and Paris) 107–21.
Symeonoglou, S.	1973	*Kadmeia I: Mycenaean Finds from Thebes, Greece. Excavation at 14 Oedipus St.* SIMA 35 (Göteborg).
Tournavitou, I.	1995	*The "Ivory Houses" at Mycenae*. BSA Suppl. vol. 24 (London).
	1997	'Arts and crafts: contrasts and comparison between neopalatial and "Mycenaean" Crete. The case of ivory', in J. Driessen and A. Farnoux (eds.), *La Crète Mycénienne*. BCH Suppl. vol. 30 (Paris) 445–54.
Voutsaki, S.	2000	'Economic control, power and prestige in the Mycenaean world: the archaeological evidence', in S. Voutsaki and J. Killen (eds.), *Economy and Politics in the Mycenaean Palace States*. Cambridge Philological Society Suppl. vol. 27 (Cambridge) 195–213.

Wardle, K. A. and Wardle, D.	1997	*The Mycenaean World* (Bristol).
Wiencke, M. H.	1998	'Mycenaean Lerna', *Hesperia* 67, 125–229.
Xenaki-Sakellariou, A.	1985	*Oi thalamotoi taphoi ton Mykenon. Anaskaphes Chr. Tsounta (1887–1898)* (Paris).

CONTEXT, POTTERY AND PHOTOGRAPHIC INFORMATION (Revised 27 May 1994)

INDEX OF CODE LISTS AND ABBREVIATIONS

A) Phase Codes (The first two digits of each code denote phase, the second two context within phase)

01..	Neolithic	= I	in Fasc. 1 p. 7
02..	Early Helladic	= II	in Fasc. 1 p. 8
03..	Middle Helladic	= III	in Fasc. 1 p. 8
04..	Prehistoric cemetery (MH > LH II)	= IV	in Fasc. 1 p. 8
05..	LH IIIA	= V	in Fasc. 1 p. 8
06..	Terrace fill below LH IIIB structures	= VI	in Fasc. 1 p. 8
065..	Construction in LH IIIB	= VIB*	
07..	Destruction in mid-LH IIIB, ? as a result of earthquake	= VII	in Fasc. 1 p. 9
08..	Destruction at end of LH IIIB 2, with widespread fire	= VIII	in Fasc. 1 p. 10
09..	Early LH IIIC	= IX	in Fasc. 1 p. 11
10..	Early–Tower phases of LH IIIC	= X	in Fasc. 1 p. 11
11..	Advanced and developed phases of LH IIIC	= XI	in Fasc. 1 p. 11
12..	Wash levels and graves, final LH IIIC, Sub-Mycenaean, Protogeometric		
13..	Geometric > Classical	= XIII	in Fasc. 1 p. 11
14..	Hellenistic	= XIV	in Fasc. 1 p. 11
15..	Surface		

* Not separately described in Fasc. 1

B) Contexts within Phases

(These codes have been applied as consistently as possible regardless of phase but variations will arise depending on the stratigraphic circumstances of each. The order is where possible a logical one, but already the study of individual phases has required the introduction of additional definitions. For simplicity, these have been allotted to vacant codes without changing those already determined.)

..00	Apparently this phase, (often not yet studied)			
..05	Deliberate infill			
Construction				
..10	Not further subdivisible		..11	Fill below floors
..12	In walls/built features		..13	Below walls/features
..14	Fill behind walls		..15	In floor 1
..16	In beam slots or cuttings		..17	In (fallen) ceiling/upper floor
..18	Levelling/terracing below walls & floors		..19	Deliberate foundation deposit
Use/Alterations				
..20	General (not further definable)		..21	On floor 1 and in drains
..22	Between floor 1 and 2		..23	On floor 2
..24	Between floor 2 and 3		..25	In floor 2
..26	On floor 3		..27	Accumulated debris
..28	Accumulated debris in secondary context		..29	Deliberate pit-fill
Destruction/Abandonment				
..30	General		..31	Floor deposit
..32	Initial collapse including earth and mudbrick		..33	Calcined debris
..34	Upper fill		..35	Later collapse and wash
..39	Destruction debris in secondary context			

Disuse
..40
Disturbance
..49
(Codes from ..50 will be used, if necessary, for chronological divisions of phases already defined. E.g. 0661 = fill below floors of phase 065 [VIB]).

C) Abbreviations for Periods and Pottery Ranges

Neo	Neolithic		EH	Early Helladic
MH	Middle Helladic		I	Late Helladic I
II	Late Helladic II		A1	Late Helladic IIIA 1
A2	Late Helladic IIIA 2		B1	Late Helladic IIIB 1
B2	Late Helladic IIIB 2		Ce	Late Helladic IIIC Early
Ct	Late Helladic IIIC Tower		Cd	Late Helladic IIIC Developed
Ca	Late Helladic IIIC Advanced		Cf	Late Helladic IIIC Final
SM	Sub-Mycenaean		PG	Protogeometric
Geom	Geometric		PCor	Protocorinthian
Arch	Archaic		Class	Classical
Hell	Hellenistic		PM	Post-Mycenaean

The following abbreviations apply to pottery only:

XS	Surface, useless for dating		XM	Mixed
Y	Undiagnostic and datable only by context			

e.g.

XS(MH)	Surface but chiefly MH		XM(MH)	Mixed but chiefly MH
Y(?MH)	Undiagnostic but possibly with MH			

All pottery is recorded with a total span (*i.e.* Neo > Hell) with note of important components or points of special interest.

Note: LH IIIC Early phase and part of Tower phase now equal LH IIIC *early* in P.A. Mountjoy, *Mycenaean Decorated Pottery* (*MDP*) pp. 134–54. The rest of LH IIIC Tower phase and Developed and Advanced phases now equal LH IIIC *middle* in *MDP* pp. 155–80. LH IIIC Final phase now equals LH IIIC *late* in *MDP* (NB. her definition of LH IIIC late and Sub-Mycenaean p. 181).

D) Pottery sorting grades (Where given)

1	Fully sorted and recorded, available for checking
2	Fully sorted but in early years and partially available for checking
3	Sorted in early years and only partially available for checking (not fully reliable)
4	Preliminary sorting only, good; available for checking
5	Preliminary sorting only, very brief; available for checking
6	Sorted, not available for checking (not fully reliable)
*	to any category = reworked in later study
-	to any category = badly sorted

PHOTOGRAPHIC ARCHIVE

Negatives taken during the excavation and study which form part of the Mycenae archive are identified as follows:

60/35/11/5	1960/35mm format/roll 11/frame 5.
69-R/6/9	1969-120 format (6cm – Rollei camera)/roll 6/frame 9.